Amongst the long-needed intersection between education and decolonization, this book offers that rare mix of theory intertwined with action. Darder makes clear that to decolonize can happen in myriad ways, but not without intention, connection, and a stance of learning.

Professor Leigh Patel, Associate Dean for Equity and Justice, School of Education, University of Pittsburgh

Decolonizing Interpretive Research audaciously brings to the fore subaltern voices that not only interrogate so-called objective lenses used to research 'the other,' but also offers emancipatory, humanistic, and organic ways in which the oppressed can document and tell their stories. This is a cutting-edge book that challenges western research orthodoxies while transcending disciplinary boundaries.

Professor Pierre W. Orelus, Associate Professor and Department Chair, School of Education, Fairfield University

Decolonizing Interpretive Research: A Subaltern Methodology for Social Change brings the literature of critical, anti-colonial, postcolonial studies to bear on the process and methods of research in a manner that enacts scholarly production as social action. Antonia Darder – as teacher – foregrounds the work of her students, dismantling the hierarchies of voice and power. Together they engage research as a communal process, working as 'revolutionary partners' pushing through and against established limits of how research is defined. The dissident voices of the students peel back layers of the colonial matrix with each chapter; their words flowing as affirmations of social change in the making.

Professor Sandy Grande, Chair of the Education Department, Connecticut College

DECOLONIZING INTERPRETIVE RESEARCH

To what extent do Western political and economic interests distort perceptions and affect the Western production of research about the other? The concept of 'colonializing epistemologies' describes how knowledges outside the Western purview are often not only rendered invisible but either absorbed or destroyed.

Decolonizing Interpretive Research outlines a form of oppositional study that undertakes a critical analysis of bodies of knowledge in any field that engages with issues related to the lives and survival of those deemed as other. It focuses on creating intellectual spaces that will facilitate new readings of the world and lead toward change, both in theory and practice. The book begins by conceptualizing the various aspects of the decolonizing interpretive research approach for the reader, and the following six chapters each focus on one of these issues, grounded in a specific decolonizing interpretive study.

With a foreword by Linda Tuhiwai Smith, this book will allow readers to not only engage with the conceptual framework of this decolonizing methodology but will also give them access to examples of how the methodology has informed decolonizing interpretive studies in practice.

Antonia Darder holds the Leavey Endowed Chair of Ethics and Moral Leadership at Loyola Marymount University and is Distinguished Visiting Faculty at the University of Johannesburg. She has published numerous books and her work focuses on political questions and ethical concerns linked to racism, class inequalities, language rights, critical pedagogy, cultural studies, and Latino education. More recently, her work has sought to contend with pedagogical questions of the body and the persistent impact of coloniality on community leadership and empowerment.

DECOLONIZING INTERPRETIVE RESEARCH

A Subaltern Methodology for Social Change

Edited by Antonia Darder

Routledge
Taylor & Francis Group

LONDON AND NEW YORK

First published 2019
by Routledge
2 Park Square, Milton Park, Abingdon, Oxon OX14 4RN

and by Routledge
52 Vanderbilt Avenue, New York, NY 10017

Routledge is an imprint of the Taylor & Francis Group, an informa business

British Library Cataloguing in Publication Data
A catalogue record for this book is available from the British Library

Library of Congress Cataloging-in-Publication Data
Names: Darder, Antonia, editor.
Title: Decolonizing interpretive research : a subaltern methodology for social change / edited by Antonia Darder.
Description: Abingdon, Oxon ; New York, NY : Routledge, 2019. | Includes bibliographical references and index.
Identifiers: LCCN 2019004032| ISBN 9781138486607 (hardback) | ISBN 9781138486614 (pbk.) | ISBN 9781351045070 (ebook)
Subjects: LCSH: Critical pedagogy. | Knowledge, Theory of. | Education--Research. | Social change.
Classification: LCC LC196 .D43 2019 | DDC 121--dc23
LC record available at https://lccn.loc.gov/2019004032

ISBN: 978-1-138-48660-7 (hbk)
ISBN: 978-1-138-48661-4 (pbk)
ISBN: 978-1-351-04507-0 (ebk)

Typeset in Bembo
by Taylor & Francis Books

CONTENTS

CONTRIBUTORS

Emily Estioco Bautista holds an Ed.D. in Educational Leadership for Social Justice from Loyola Marymount University. She is a former high school social studies teacher and the current Director of Curriculum and Instruction for Transformation and Assistant Principal at YouthBuild Charter School of California. She is a founding member of the People's Education Movement based in Los Angeles. As a scholar activist, her scholarship is informed by her personal experience as a student leader and organizer, as she applies critical, decolonizing, and healing justice lenses to explore, engage, and create transformative possibilities in intergenerational organizing and youth movements.

Kenzo Bergeron holds an Ed.D. in Education Leadership for Social Justice from Loyola Marymount University. Currently, he is the lead mathematics specialist at Village School, California. Bergeron's research explores the intersection of psychology and education as they work to negatively impact subaltern populations. He is the author of *Challenging the Cult of Self-Esteem in Education: Education, Psychology, and the Subaltern Self*.

Antonia Darder, born in Puerto Rico, is a distinguished international critical educational scholar. She is a public intellectual, educator, writer, activist, and artist. Darder holds the Leavey Presidential Endowed Chair of Ethics and Moral Leadership at Loyola Marymount University, Los Angeles; is Distinguished Visiting Professor of Education at the University of Johannesburg; and is Professor Emerita of Education Policy, Organization, and Leadership at the University of Illinois Urbana Champaign. She is an American Educational Research Association Fellow and recipient of the AERA Scholars of Color Lifetime Contribution Award. She is the author of numerous books and articles in the field, including *Culture and Power in the Classroom* (20th anniversary edition), *Reinventing Paulo Freire: A Pedagogy of*

Love, A Dissident Voice: Essays on Culture, Pedagogy, and Power, Freire and Education, and *The Student Guide to Freire's Pedagogy of the Oppressed.*

Kortney Hernandez holds an Ed.D. in Educational Leadership for Social Justice, a Master of Arts in Early Childhood Education, and a Bachelor of Arts in Criminology, Law and Society. In her book *Service Learning as a Political Act in Education,* she critically engages the phenomenon of service learning/community engagement through a bicultural decolonizing epistemological lens.

João Paraskeva is a professor in the doctoral program in Education Leadership and Policy Studies, Masters of Public Policy and Masters of Arts and Teaching at the University of Massachusetts, Dartmouth. A former middle school and high school teacher in the southern Africa region he was also a professor at the University of Minho Portugal, Honorary Fellow of the University of Wisconsin Madison, Visiting Professor at the University of La Coruna, Spain, Federal University of Pelotas, Brazil, University of Florence, Italy, and Miami University, Oxford, Ohio. He is the author of *Curriculum Epistemicides, Curriculum: Whose Internationalization,* and *Itinerant Curriculum Theory.*

Bibinaz Pirayesh earned a B.S. in Neuroscience and Education from the University of Pittsburg, an M.A. in Developmental Psychology from Columbia University and an Ed.D. in Educational Leadership for Social Justice from Loyola Marymount University, where she is a clinical faculty involved with a number of service organizations, including the Association of Educational Therapists where she serves as Chair of Research. She has worked as a learning specialist and educational therapist in private practice for over a decade.

Terrelle Billy Sales is Assistant Professor of Graduate Education for Single Subject Credential Candidates at Vanguard University of Southern California. He earned an Ed.D. in Educational Leadership for Social Justice from Loyola Marymount University. His research interests include the application of the principles of Liberation Theology and Critical Pedagogy in both spiritual and educational contexts. His most recent study looked at the praxis of Jesus Christ's pedagogy and the Christocentric intersectionality of Critical Pedagogy and Liberation Theology and its implications for educators, researchers, leaders, and clergy.

Linda Tuhiwai Smith (Ngāti Awa and Ngāti Porou, Māori) is a scholar of education and critic of persistent colonialism in academic teaching and research. She is best known for her groundbreaking 1999 book, *Decolonizing Methodologies.* Here, Smith traced the history of scientific knowledge as it developed through racist practices and the exploitation of indigenous peoples, and asserts a challenging vision for how research and education can be used to confront colonialism and oppression. Re-released in 2012, the book launched a wave of indigenous-led critiques of academic power and proposals for indigenized methodological interventions.

FOREWORD

Linda Tuhiwai Smith

A still too common scenario for me is that a Māori doctoral student asks to see me so she can discuss issues with her research. She comes to my office, sits down and cries. She is not one of my own doctoral students but is from another faculty and with a supervision team who are not Māori, may not have done their own research in New Zealand, and have little understanding or sympathy for the Māori context. The student's concerns are ones I continue to hear such as "there is no such thing as an Indigenous methodology" or "decolonizing methodologies are irrelevant in today's educational settings," or "there is no need to bring up historical issues of colonization because that's in the past," or the one that makes me laugh, "Linda is not on our faculty so you can't talk to her as we have our own methods here." Those are the general comments but then there are more specific ones such as "if you want to have an academic career you need to stick to mainstream theories," or, "I come from a multicultural country so I understand your peoples' issues," and, "you cannot reference those researchers (Indigenous, critical, decolonial ones) because they are only writing about a narrow field."

This happens in a university widely known for its strengths in Māori and Indigenous Studies. While Māori staff are positioned across the university, we are still a minority and there are not enough of us to supervise students from our Māori communities. These recurring scenarios reinforce the overpowering arrogance and privilege of academic faculty to define, frame, and order knowledge and determine what matters for doctoral students who in our system are expected to produce research that extends the boundaries of the known. Of course, we are not unique in that respect as I meet doctoral students from Indigenous and diverse communities across the world who share similar frustrations and tears.

In this book, Antonia Darder brings together a group of contributors that come from the kinds of places that resonate with the experiences of students from my own Indigenous communities in Aotearoa, New Zealand. This book has come from a communal process that has supported the contributors to express their own ideas and speak to the research they want to do. As Bibinaz Pirayesh writes in Chapter 5, she came to her studies "almost in secret" and it was only through honoring her own bicultural background and perspective that she could begin to see the lack of critical literature that comes from her area and the dominance of literature that excludes and erases the perspectives that come from other communities. The dominant literature not only excludes and defines fields of knowledge but crowds out any other ways to know, indeed any other language, terminology, theoretical, and philosophical diversities. There is never polite wriggle room in the crowded spaces of colonial knowledge production for the voices of the Other. Decolonizing knowledges is partly about elbowing some of those dominant discourses out of the way, clearing spaces and creating networks and hubs of scholars who can begin to talk rather than whisper, interpret critically rather than see the world through the gaze of imperial authority.

In Part I, Antonia lays out the central methodological arguments for decolonizing approaches to interpretive research in education and why these approaches are necessary and urgent. The problem with so many of the dominant theories of educational research is they have spectacularly failed to transform the lives of subaltern communities and have instead reinforced privilege and inequalities across all developed and developing countries. Decolonizing approaches unsettle the settled in order, as Antonia argues, to offer new insights, develop new theories that offer transforming possibilities for our communities. Antonia here clearly lays out some of the critical concepts necessary for decolonizing interpretive research, such as the importance of understanding cultural politics, political economy, the historicity of knowledge, ideology, hegemony, critique, counter-hegemony, conscientization, subaltern voice, and other fundamental organizing ideas in a decolonizing approach. This is superbly helpful for readers grappling with decolonizing research more broadly.

Antonia also introduces and releases the voices of major scholars in the decolonizing fields writing from different contexts and perspectives whose work profoundly shapes our understandings of colonialism and cultural imperialism and the complex work of decolonizing education. I see many of these scholars as "my friends and mentors" even though I don't actually know most of them. Like for the contributors in this book, I feel that my friends and mentors lived in my head during my doctoral journey and beyond. They gave me a language, a way to imagine something I could not voice in education, a way to see my own reality through a different lens. As Kortney Hernandez argues in Chapter 2, these writers provide a language that can wake up the imagination and release the voice that has often been silenced within the mainstream educational system. Of course, this voice can come bursting, bubbling, tumbling out in an undisciplined and release of mixed up excitement and naivety; so, learning to use it requires a process of learning how to use the tools and resources with radical compassion.

In Chapter 3, Emily Estioco Bautista reminds us of the significance of Paulo Freire's work in bringing the challenge of decolonization right down into classrooms and pedagogical practices. Emily draws the connection between Freire's ideas into her study of social movements and youth organizing pedagogies. She discusses the dimensions of colonial control, from control of land to control of knowledge and the parallel processes for instilling colonial systems of control and hegemony. Colonial education, as she argues, upheld and modelled Western ideations of civilization, knowledge, racial hierarchies, and culture. Kenzo Begeron's introduction to Chapter 4 provides a narrative of awakening the decolonizing spirit through an "accidental on purpose" confrontation with one's own lived experience. I appreciated the transparency of the initial steps being described, as I can see some of my own students reacting to this with their own narratives. As one of my newer doctoral graduates said, once she took the first steps into Indigenous Kaupapa Māori methodology, "there is no going back." Kenzo's decolonial critique of self-esteem theory is an excellent example of how a decolonizing analysis can reinterpret a taken for granted idea and offer new insights. In Chapter 6, Terrelle Billy Sales writes powerfully about identifying as Black and Christian and the "ethereal struggle to develop an empowered identity." Terrelle gets to the heart of the contradictions, complexities, and new identities that have to be forged in a colonial context. He writes of the "deep yearning for an educational experience that affirms his identity and cultivates his curiosity and spiritual formation." Terrelle re-reads education through the idea of the emancipatory pedagogy of Jesus Christ and focuses on the human moment, conscientization, and the principle of love.

It is with great excitement then that I offer this foreword, as it is vitally important that doctoral students from diverse communities and backgrounds, especially from those who have been excluded or erased from the academy, have access to texts such as this book that affirms identities and aspirations and provides critical ways of thinking and being as students in doctoral programs. It is important that doctoral students do work that is critical, decolonizing, transforming, and meaningful to the communities they come from. To do this they need supervisors, teachers, mentors, and colleagues who not only have understanding and compassion, but who can also provide critical language, arguments, theories, methods, and approaches. They need teachers and mentors who can introduce them to networks of leading scholars working in these spaces. They need people who can support them to not only do good critical decolonizing work, but who can also help them be good critical decolonizing scholars, activists, educators, and human beings. Antonia Darder has done exactly this, in that she has produced with her colleagues an excellent decolonizing resource that introduces important theories, language, and ways of writing for those working in interpretive research spaces.

PREFACE

This book emerged from a communal process with doctoral students from subaltern communities, who were experiencing much frustration as they navigated the doctoral research sphere. Generally, they were given two options: to do a quantitative study or to do a qualitative study. In both instances, they were expected to find willing subjects to participate in their study. In many instances, students felt tremendous trepidation with research designs that sought "voices" of others, while their own voices were being silenced. They came to the table with an urgent sense that a necessary critique had to be made within their spheres of work, given the manner in which theories in the field of education continue to replicate a positivist perspective, even when appropriating voices of the other. Here I am speaking about doctoral students of color who were highly insightful and perceptive about the oppression at work in their world and who were committed to doing the kind of scholarship that could assist us in shifting consciousness about how we understood educational practices. In all instances, students were feeling corralled to enact oppressive research designs that further colonized them and their potential participants. Moreover, these were subaltern human beings with a lived history of educational practice, whose sensibilities and ways of thinking moved them politically and philosophically to consider how repressive theories might be transformed in ways that might also mobilize new consciousness and collaborations toward transforming practices in the field.

Unfortunately, in many academic settings, doctoral students are infantilized and, more so, if these students are members of indigenous or subaltern communities. This is further intensified if they hail from working-class communities of color, where they obviously lack the social and academic pedigree of the elite and privileged student. The deficit lens that has generally accompanied their educational journeys is recognized only too well by those who have traversed the path to doctoral degree, often as the first in their families to receive an advanced degree of any kind. In this case, perceptions and judgments are tied to stereotypical notions that these students are insufficiently prepared to participate in the ambitious project of critiquing and transforming educational theory. In the process, they were often met with "well-meaning" disrespect and a professional tendency to expertly silence their dissident voices.

Hence, the work reflected in this book arose from a deep commitment to listening very closely, with respect and humility, to the thoughts, passions, and struggles doctoral students were waging within the research process. Relating here very closely with my own experience through academia, I decided to seek an alternative and collective approach that would not only respect their cultural and political insights, but also more deliberately nurture their emancipatory passion to make a difference in the world. With this impetus, I began to consider how interpretive research—often reserved for philosophy, history, and other more privileged disciplines and less applied fields—might be brought into play within education, in ways that could support a larger decolonizing political project. It was then from this work with former doctoral students, five whose work is featured in this volume, that this decolonizing interpretive methodology was born. Hence, its origins are communal and relational, emerging from actual struggles faced and pursuing ways to open the field of research engagement for advanced subaltern students of education that would draw upon their thirst for justice and honor their lived histories of struggle.

This book is therefore a result of praxis—a decolonizing praxis often denied or hidden, which requires doctoral students and their advisors, as revolutionary partners, to push against the Eurocentric limitations of how we define research, in order to create an expanded field of engagement. Through such a process, an approach was forged that supported the efforts of developing subaltern researchers to critically engage the literature in the field in critical ways—ways that unveil its shortcomings and oppressive epistemological directions, as the decolonizing researcher simultaneously sought to bring into being a new way of seeing social phenomena that could result in a more just understanding of subaltern social and material needs and its meaning to the practice of education. This required that decolonizing interpretive researchers tarry through unknown and uncertain dimensions of the work, which would often cause them to painfully doubt and question their own thinking, given the voluminous literature that seemed to authoritatively counter their perceptions and that often sought to take them away from the center of their focus: to arrive at a decolonizing understanding that could challenge the commonsense ideas supported by so-called evidence-based approaches to research in the field.

As the reader may have already assumed, this book is not a recipe for how to conduct decolonizing interpretive research, but rather provides an example of the experiences and ideas linked to an approach to knowledge construction, within a particular context, which pushed against the colonizing formations so often taken for granted within graduate educational studies. It is, instead, a response to the paralysis doctoral students often experience in the face of contemporary colonizing research that continues to be shaped by an epistemology of conquest and accumulation. Moreover, I cannot emphasize enough that this book is the outcome of engaging the actual experiences of developing subaltern educational scholars whose perspectives were often silenced and invisibilized in their classes by well-meaning faculty, who were simply unprepared to understand their sensibilities or support them in expressing and centering their subaltern voices. As such, the book emerges from radical hope and a commitment to shed light on aspects of a decolonizing interpretive approach that reflects a praxis of knowledge production that deliberately seeks to respect and center the voices and sensibilities of subaltern researchers, as well as critically imagine new ways of knowing the world.

The decolonizing research approach discussed in this book also comes from a stubborn refusal to accept the zero-sum sensibilities that are shrouded in traditional research approaches and the too often deficient portrayal of subaltern doctoral students, particularly those who seek to push the boundaries of a mainstream or colonizing ethos of reality. As such, this work also reflects a politically determined refusal to surrender the academic field of knowledge construction and, instead, engage it as a deeply contested terrain of struggle, which is central to the shifting of consciousness and the transformation of social and material conditions in the world. In other words, how we make sense of the world has a direct impact on material relations and on our capacity for participation in social change.

With this in mind, it is important that we recognized how the meaning of social change particularly with respect to subaltern communities, has been heavily reified, conflated, and rendered one-dimensional; reduced often to mean only street protesting, grassroots political work, or working within community organizations. Consequently, often the work of subaltern intellectuals has been marginalized and vilified, given the colonizing culture of the academy and society, which leaves many in our communities suspicious (and rightly so) of any knowledge production derived from participation within universities. Yet, we cannot pretend there are not good reasons for this suspicion, given the manner in which neocolonial actors have betrayed many of our revolutionary dreams. However, surrendering this sphere of struggle, at this time, does not seem to be in the interest of subaltern communities, in that if we do not define our existence, there will be those who have no hesitation defining it for us.

The concept of social change I'm advocating here acknowledges unapologetically that the critical praxis that surrounds decolonizing interpretive research is, in fact, a form of social action; in that it is grounded in a decolonizing view of knowledge as always relational and tied to human social action, rather than as autonomous and transcendent. Hence, no one owns knowledge. This is a view of knowledge that directly counters the limiting property relations akin to colonialism and capitalism. Moreover, inherent to subaltern sensibilities and our decolonial purpose is a deep commitment to connect our research to other forms of social action, within spheres where the decolonizing perspectives shared here might potentially support concrete transformations not only in the field of research, but also the daily lives of our students, families, and communities. As such, the intellectual labor of navigating borderlands, shattering epistemicides, struggling to (re)make the stories of our peoples, and forging shifts in consciousness represents a necessary form of political action and, thus, constitutes a contribution to the larger political project of liberation. Furthermore, what I'm suggesting is that a decolonizing solidarity that emerges from our subalternity can potentially support our collective actions, assist us to overcome our fears, and courageously join us together to make our own destinies.

There is no question that all researchers exist within the social and material conditions that shape our lived histories; hence, this work also recognizes that we are interdependently immersed in the colonizing structures we critique. With this in mind, the methodological claims offered here transpired through a communal process of doctoral research, where young researchers involved in a dissertation writing group would consistently present their work over two years to one another and then provide each other questions and feedback consistent with a decolonizing approach to knowledge construction. In this way, the communal or relational dimension of their knowledge formation was deeply nurtured in the context of each researcher's critical engagement with the decolonizing gaps in the literature they were studying, within a counterhegemonic space that allowed them to navigate and move beyond the typical silences so often resulting from the colonizing structures of mainstream academic formation.

Lastly, I want to affirm, in particular, the powerful work of decolonizing methodology scholars such as Linda Tuhiwai Smith, Sandy Grande, Eve Tuck, Leigh Patel, Wayne Yang, João Paraskeva, and so many others, whose rigorous works over the years have been key to many of the decolonizing ideas presented here and whose books must also be read to better understand the magnitude and complexity of this political project. Through their great courage, these indigenous and subaltern scholars have worked diligently over the years to open the door for greater critical engagement with decolonizing futures. Hence, this small volume foundationally builds on their contributions in ways that speak here specifically to the labor of decolonizing interpretive research. Although, I recognize that interpretive studies represents a small sphere of educational research, the groundbreaking work that has been produced by subaltern educational scholars employing this methodology (five featured in this volume), points to the limitless possibilities for embracing decolonizing methodologies—possibilities, which although often obscured by the colonizing epistemological limitation of Western ways of knowing, can assist us to break away from the persistent chaos of coloniality and capitalism in the world today. With all this in mind, this book seeks, even in a small way, to purposefully support the dismantling of oppressive and exploitative beliefs in the field and society, as it joins with other decolonizing research efforts to set us onto new paths toward our collective liberation.

Antonia Darder
Los Angeles, California

PART I

The conceptual foundation

Many other Maori people, I was aware of, were scared of what lay in cupboards, of whose bones and whose ancestors were imprisoned in those cases.[1]

---

1   Linda Tuhiwai Smith, *Decolonizing methodologies* (London: Zed Books, 1999), p. 11.

PART I

The conceptual foundation

1

DECOLONIZING INTERPRETIVE RESEARCH

Antonia Darder

> Decolonization is a process which engages with imperialism and colonialism at multiple levels. For researchers, one of those levels is concerned with having a more critical understanding of the underlying assumptions, motivations and values which inform research practices.
>
> *(Smith, 1999)*

Decolonizing the interpretive encompasses a rigorous process of study that demands of us to "risk imagining an entirely different relationship between knowledge and reality" (Savransky, 2017, p. 18), by expanding and transforming the limits of rationality. In so doing, we labor toward the development of counterhegemonic forms of thinking and reflecting upon the world, so to better grasp the colonizing impact of current social and material relations of power at work in the lives of subaltern populations. In turn, decolonizing interpretive research designs aim to demystify the artificial limits of colonizing and racialized formations and economic hierarchies of domination, viewing all languages and cultures as not only significant to our planetary survival but also open to critical discernment, with respect to their oppressive or decolonizing impact on communities.

Although critical influences inform a variety of qualitative approaches, including critical ethnographies, critical narratives, and indigenous research modalities, the critical discussion here is focused on a decolonizing interpretive approach, in that it is often the least well defined, understood, or discussed in research methods courses within most educational studies programs. This may be the case because interpretive theory building is often, overtly or covertly, discouraged in educational research and only seldom offered up as a viable alternative, particularly to graduate indigenous or subaltern students in the field who are often not perceived as sufficiently capable of such depth of analysis—whether openly acknowledged or not. Yet, it is significant to note that despite this traditional deficit notion, much of the decolonizing interpretive research currently found in the field has actually emerged directly from the doctoral studies of subaltern scholars.

Yet, it cannot be ignored that there is "very real ambivalence in Western universities about the legitimacy of indigenous [and subaltern] knowledge and the role of indigenous [and other subaltern] intellectuals" (Mutua & Swadener, 2004, p. 10). This same ambivalence is also extended toward our form of knowledge production. As such, common critiques of decolonizing interpretive research can include concerns that it is purely abstract work, which fails to provide a sufficiently challenging research experience, produce practical or useful knowledge, or include the voices of the oppressed. Of the first line of critique, decolonizing interpretive research is absolutely by no means a less significant research design or less rigorous. In fact, according to Rudestam and Newton (2007):

> Original theoretical contributions are a profound intellectual challenge ... If you know an area of inquiry inside out and are intimately familiar with the issues and controversies in the field, you have the chance to contribute a new theory ... If you do choose to pursue a theoretical [approach], you will be expected to argue from the literature that there is a different way of understanding a phenomenon than has heretofore been presented. Some of the more viable theoretical dissertations in the social sciences are those that bring together or integrate two previously distinct areas.
>
> *(pp. 54–55)*

About concerns that a decolonizing approach is less rigorous, due to its expressed political and cultural subjectivity, there are a few things that must be understood. Rigor is the outcome of developing an intellectual capacity to engage critically and move with depth into different aspects and dimensions of an issue or problem that one is studying and to do this both systematically and creatively. However, within the context of a decolonizing interpretive analysis, critical subaltern researchers must enact these critical skills in a manner that consistently contends with the link between theory and practice and within their own labor as educators and researchers out in the world. Academic rigor within the context of a decolonizing interpretive research design must be understood then as not only a cognitive or abstract process of analysis. Rather, it also entails a deeply physical, emotional, and spiritual activity for subaltern researchers; which, when practiced consistently, allows them to become more integral human beings, through a creative epistemological process of what Freire called problematization and radicalization (Darder, 2015)—an empowering process of knowledge construction that is also deeply rooted in the researcher's worldview.

On the second criticism relative to practicality or usefulness, a decolonizing interpretive design is meant to generate new insights or develop a new theory from the richness of a detailed comparison of bodies of existing literature related to both theory and practice. This is essential if critical subaltern researchers are to disrupt and deliberately shift the hegemonic understanding of a social or educational phenomenon and move beyond traditional views of schooling and society. This inherently implies that a different practice must ensue, given the shift in the epistemological framework that both defines the problem and posits alternatives for future liberatory practice. For example, this calls for critical approaches that move beyond the deceptive quantophrenia of positivism, which counter the tendency to embrace quantification of all social phenomenon and a tyrannous discourse of evidence-based, even among qualitative researchers. This traditional privileging of a scientific epistemology of knowledge construction, wittingly or unwittingly, disrupts our ability to delve deeper into the human meanings and conditions that result in oppression and its disastrous consequences on oppressed populations. Decolonizing methodologies are in direct opposition to this tendency in education and the social sciences. It is for this reason that Fanon insists, "But the native intellectual who wishes to create an authentic work ... must realize that the truths of a nation are in the first place its realities. [They] must go on until [they have] found the seething pot out of which the learning of the future will emerge" (1967, p. 223). This *seething pot* is precisely that decolonizing interpretive knowledge that can support a shift in social consciousness, social relationships, and social structures in the interest of economic and cultural democracy.

Further, there is the often-voiced and well-meaning concern about the "absence of voices" with respect to interpretive research. Decolonizing interpretive research, however, signals an analysis that inherently requires a formidable decolonizing process of deductive analysis—an inferential analysis deeply anchored upon the a priori communal knowledge of the subaltern voices emerging from the communities in which they labor (Darder, 2012). This is what it means to "know an area of inquiry inside out and [be] intimately familiar with the issues and controversies" (Rudestam & Newton, 2007, pp. 54–55) that exist within the communal cultural context. However, Grosfoguel (2011) rightly asserts that "this is not only a question about social values in knowledge production or the fact that our knowledge is always partial. The main point here is the locus of enunciation, that is, the geo-political and body-political location of the subject that speaks" (p. 4).

Accordingly, research conclusions—although assumed in traditional definitions of interpretive research to be a process of individual production or a unilateral voice (due to the individualistic assumptions of humanness and knowledge construction inherent in the episteme of the West)—are derived from subaltern researchers' sense of kinship, as well as consistent and ongoing critical engagement with the collective voices of fellow colonized or subaltern subjects within their communal interactions. Decolonizing interpretive research then is inextricably tied to the communal subaltern voice (or the "I am because we are" voice), which sits and remains ever at the center of this communally informed interpretive analysis. This radical understanding of the subaltern voice echoes Freire's notion that the emancipatory knowledge of the researcher must emerge from an intimacy with "the empirical knowledge of the people" (Freire, 2012, p. 181). It is from whence that the subaltern decolonizing researcher knows herself or himself, as part and parcel, with the people, while also recognizing that we always speak from a particular location in the structure of power (Dussel, 1977, cited in Grosfoguel, 2011).

Hence, the overarching purpose of a decolonizing interpretive methodology is to provide an emancipatory reformulation of the conceptual or ideological interrelationships that exist between theoretical explanations and practical applications from a particular location within a specific field or area of study. In light of this purpose, the development of theory (or a theory building emphasis) must be understood here as primarily an integrative process. This to say, it will either produce a new or reformulated decolonizing framework for consideration in some aspect of human phenomenon or demonstrate the ways in which existing theoretical constructs in the field do (or do not) coincide with decolonizing epistemological requirements or are in sync with other counterhegemonic theoretical perspectives (i.e., critical, feminist, queer, etc.). Important to this rearticulation is a sound decolonizing analysis and interpretation that distinctly demonstrates what theoretical, structural, and practical transformations would be necessary in the process of effectively positing decolonizing conclusions that may arise from such a study.

Some decolonizing interpretive research aims might include mounting or extending a decolonizing framework into areas in which it had previously not been applied, by applying the insights garnered from a critical interrogation of traditional perspectives. Or, it might entail a decolonizing research design that combines several emancipatory lenses of analysis into a single decolonizing conceptual framework or that demonstrates previously unacknowledged links between theoretical systems that point to decolonizing claims. On another note, it may encompass the introduction of an existing decolonizing conceptual framework from another field (e.g., theology, science, psychology, etc.) into education, with appropriate deconstructions, modifications, and extensions to make it meaningful within a new decolonizing intellectual and practical space. And, lastly, this methodological design can engage a variety of more specific decolonizing theoretical discussions related to a specific phenomenon that, by so doing, provides new critical insights related to theory and practice, by integrating concepts and perspectives derived from several critical perspectives (e.g., racialization, queer studies, and disability theories), which now are taken up through a decolonizing interpretive lens responsive to challenges, limits, contestations, and possibilities.

Key to this work is also the examination and interrogation of existing bodies of literature that focus on the topic of study, which provide empirical support and point to the need for a decolonizing approach in understanding, deconstructing, and recreating the central problem or question that drives the study. Moreover, a critical interpretive design provides a place for a detailed presentation of the new theoretical construct of analysis, which must emerge from a comparative decolonizing analysis of existing bodies of literature related to the central question, carefully substantiating the claims made through a decolonizing process of critical reinterpretation. Such a study concludes by summarizing the process of critical analysis and moving toward a decolonizing theoretical position or emancipatory framework, considering the implications for educational practices and policy formulation that would be consistent with a new decolonizing perspective, with a clear discussion of how it differs with its hegemonic counterpart.

Hence, wherever possible, appropriate recommendations related to emancipatory pedagogy, curriculum, leadership, and/or educational policy or community practices can be offered, linking these in lucid and consistent ways to the structural and practical transformations required to enact and embody a decolonizing approach, as well as political recommendations derived from the analysis. Moreover, a decolonizing interpretive approach to research integrates a critical lens of analysis across the study, arranging discussions along a new logical evolution of the argument, according to the relationship of topics that impact this evolution, rather than by chronology. That is, discussions unfold decolonizing forms of knowledge through a subaltern analysis of existing bodies of literature pertinent to the topic of study and brushing these constantly against the existing emancipatory literature and the subaltern knowledge held by the author—all which help open the field to reinvention. The critical understanding that emerges from this decolonizing approach to research can be further demonstrated through the presentation of new curriculum, theoretical approaches, knowledge practices, or political strategies that move the field into more emancipatory and just ways of knowing and reading the world.

Critical influences

> Decolonizing concepts within the context of research have often emerged out of a foundation of critique: a critical analysis of the ways in which colonialism still affects the way the world is viewed.
>
> *(Alcoff, 2007)*

In many instances, critical influences have served to support the epistemological creativity, imagination, questioning, doubting, and risk-taking necessary to employing this research approach. This supports a research design that incorporates the decolonizing researcher as an unapologetically political participant, whose knowledge is understood *a priori* as partial, unfinished, and deeply informed by historical, economic, and cultural configurations of the changing social and material conditions of our time. Moreover, "by applying a critical pedagogical lens within research, we create an empowering qualitative research, which expands, contracts, grows, and questions itself within the theory and practice examined" (Kincheloe et al., 2017, p. 243). As the discussion above suggests, this articulation of decolonizing interpretive research draws upon critical influences of knowledge construction (Darder et al., 2017; Darder, 2012), in concert with the radical epistemological tradition of critical social theory that was later reformulated by radical educational theorists as critical pedagogy.[1]

Moreover, as we often find in anticolonial analyses of the south (i.e., Dussel, 2003, 2013; Mignolo, 2007; Santos, 2005; Quijano, 2000 and others), critical influences inform the decolonizing epistemological underpinnings of this interpretive research approach. At the heart, these critical influences counter classical positivist approaches to the study of human phenomenon. They point us toward dismantling traditional Western philosophical assumptions and values of empiricism associated with hegemonic forms of knowledge construction. These include research conclusions that privilege reasoning shaped by an underlying belief in the superiority of an either/or, linear, reductionist, hierarchical, concrete, universalist, object/subject or nature/human binary, and neutral, decontextualized, ahistorical, and apolitical methodologies in the construction of claims related to human phenomenon.

Accordingly, a decolonizing interpretive approach to knowledge construction is often understood as a meta-process of investigation, in that it involves the interrogation and disruption of currently held values, beliefs, and assumptions, and, from this systematic interrogation and disruption, a deliberate and conscious move toward a decolonizing reformulation of how the histories, experiences, and lives of oppressed populations are understood. This entails a rigorous process aimed at exposing the manner in which traditional research aims to conceal "the location of the subject of enunciation" and how "European/American colonial expansion and domination [is] able to construct a hierarchy of superior and inferior knowledge and, thus, of superior and inferior people around the world" (Grosfoguel, 2011, p. 6). Again, this decolonizing research methodology is intentionally meant to challenge colonizing social structures that perpetuate racialized, gendered, economic, sexual, and other forms of social exclusions that persist within education and the larger society. In the process, decolonizing interpretive research seeks to unveil and destabilize the existing structures of power that perpetuate the material and social oppression of the most vulnerable populations.

Decolonizing forms of critical inquiry do not seek to simply describe or interpret the world based on traditional notions, but rather encompass an underlying commitment to the conceptual rethinking and transformation of norms, as a qualitative process of analysis. Major assumptions that inform this critical decolonizing process of inquiry can be linked to key influences concerned with the mediation of power relations in society; acknowledgment of the manner in which colonizing forms of social privilege and wealth stratification reproduce social and material inequalities; a recognition that all ideas or truth unfold amid particular forms of ideology; and, as such, dominant research epistemologies are implicated in the historical reproduction of colonizing forms of oppression, as well as contemporary forms of cultural and linguistic genocide.

It is worth restating that to articulate or critically define a decolonizing perspective in a definitive manner is never an easy endeavor. Accordingly, many critical scholars (Freire, 2012; Giroux, 1981, 1983; McLaren, 1986; Shor, 1987; Darder, 2012; hooks, 1994; Bauman, 1995; Carlson & Apple, 1998; Kellner, 1995; Grande, 2004; Kincheloe, 2008; Kincheloe & McLaren, 2005; Kahn, 2010) who have contributed to the development of a critical analysis of education have been reticent and, rightly so, to posit what might be perceived as a simplistic recipe for what is, in fact, a deeply complex field of study. Nevertheless, through a careful analysis of the literature in the field, we can gain a sense of the underlying critical influences that inform and drive its epistemological directions. It is from such critical pedagogical efforts, in combination with subaltern sensibilities, that a decolonizing interpretive analysis[2] can be imagined and considered. Hence, in brief, the epistemological lens that underlies decolonizing interpretive research may include a variety of aspects that are related to the following critical ideas. Moreover, it cannot be ignored that these influences often inform the textual analysis undertaken in the development of this decolonizing interpretive reformulation, in order to support and sustain a decolonizing process of social change, in both theory and practice.

Cultural politics

The majority of research is conducted and functions within a colonizing form of cultural politics that is shaped by the prescribed social norms and acceptable epistemological boundaries of what constitutes legitimate knowledge within the dominant academic arena. The aim of criticality here is then to function as both a decolonizing and democratizing force, by way of embodying an emancipatory epistemology that engages the manner in which cultural politics are implicated in the process of both domination and subordination. As such, the practice of decolonizing research is understood as a political act and encompasses a terrain of struggle where competing definitions and perspectives are tied to the control of knowledge, as well as the systematic control of social and material resources. Accordingly, the role of decolonizing interpretive researchers is understood as that of cultural workers, who recognize and interrogate intersectionalities of culture and power, particularly with respect to transforming colonizing forms of cultural politics linked to ethnicity, gender, sexuality, religion, and physical ability, imbuing their interpretive studies with the power of a decolonial imagination (Alcoff, 2007).

Political economy

Similarly, researchers traditionally are expected to function within the values and norms that sustain the political and economic interests of the powerful. Inherent in their labor is an allegiance to the hegemonic structure associated with class formation. With this in mind, the political economy and its colonizing impact upon the construction of knowledge must be clearly acknowledged and systematically interrogated within a decolonizing interpretive design. Social class, whether acknowledged or not, is central to the manner in which all researchers forge a sense of their purpose and how they understand their social location and positionality within society. As such, a colonizing system of meritocracy and economic inequalities are directly linked to the production of traditional research and, as such, wittingly or unwittingly, functions to preserve asymmetrical relations of power tied to capitalism within institutions and the society at large. Accordingly, decolonizing research approaches systematically unveil this relationship in ways that make obvious the structure and impact of material oppression on the lives of subaltern populations.

Historicity of knowledge

All knowledge is understood as historical and contextual, despite the reification of official knowledge that normalizes the dominant vantage point as natural, fixed, and commonsensical. Immutable myths linked to the conservation of the coloniality of power, for example, are challenged here by bringing the power of historicity and its unfinishedness (Freire, 1998) to bear on the study of human phenomenon. With this in mind, decolonizing researchers and their communities are understood as historical subjects who, simultaneously, shape and are shaped by the impermanent and unfolding historical conditions that shape the contemporary moment. The personal histories of decolonizing interpretive researchers are, therefore, always implicated in the research process and, because this is so, they work to define their studies of indigenous or subaltern communities upon the sensibilities that inform their lives—sensibilities grounded upon their histories of survival under colonialism and capitalist rule.

Dialectical view[3] of knowledge

Decolonizing research embraces a critical view of knowledge as dynamic and reconstructive. Hence, knowledge here exists in an epistemological field that disrupts traditional notions of absolute or pure objectivity. Instead, knowledge is grasped as contextual, social, and partial in nature. Informed by a dialectical view of knowledge, a decolonizing lens shatters traditional binaries and dichotomies (i.e., humans/nature; mind/body, etc.) and hierarchical notions (i.e., elitism, privilege) of the world, widening the field of human engagement. Within the dialectical tradition of critical theory, oppositional elements function within a continuum of tensions that confront and challenge what Freire (2012) termed "limit-situations," to open up new possibilities of interaction between human beings and the world. This speaks to epistemologies of knowledge construction where contradictory elements and tensions linked to the negation of oppositionalities are recognized, engaged, challenged, and reinvented in efforts to arrive at decolonizing possibilities.

Ideology

A decolonizing epistemology critically contends that there is always a set of ideas or ideology that shape the frame or lens by which researchers study and make sense of the world. How we understand and interpret our world and our positionality in the world determines the kind of questions we ask, how we ask them, and how we lay out the means for answering these questions through our labor as researchers. Therefore, theories and methods of research are generally linked to particular cultural/ class interests and relations of power. Important to note here is that ideology largely exists at the level of unexamined assumptions often considered to be "commonsense" or "naturally" existing. In direct contrast, a decolonizing methodology claims that research is never a neutral enterprise, in that it encompasses the values, beliefs, ethics, and contradictions at work in the mainstream of society.

Hegemony

Antonio Gramsci's (1971) notion of hegemony serves as an important critical influence in the work of decolonizing scholars. Made explicit is the construction of commonsense notions within the process of research that effectively naturalize or normalize colonizing relations of power and practices that perpetuate paternalism and deceptive notions of impartiality, shrouding hegemonic interests. This is made possible in that traditional practices of research, more often than not, serve to legitimate the existing social order through fabricated mass consensus, irrespective of contradictions and inequalities reproduced. Research practices, then, as part of an ideological apparatus (i.e., culture industry) function to preserve the status quo, through constructing knowledge claims that echo dominant beliefs and sensibilities. This control of the social sphere is said to be hegemonic, in that it is reproduced and perpetuated by the unexamined moral and intellectual leadership of researchers, who have been prepared and sanctioned by the academy as the legitimate makers of knowledge and professional experts.

Critique

Critique here entails an interrogation into the values and beliefs that sustain asymmetrical or colonizing relations of power. With this view of critique, decolonizing research works to unveil hidden epistemologies and the logic of power at work within the structure of traditional methodologies and, thus, their research claims and conclusions. In this light, decolonizing interpretive methodologies function in the interest of deconstructing and reimagining conditions for transformative practice and community sovereignty and empowerment. A deep sense of faith in the capacity of indigenous and other subaltern communities to change our current conditions and remake our destinies through a critical process of naming the politics of coloniality, problematizing our reality, and positing new possibilities for change, is supported by this critical supposition.

Counterhegemony

In the context of a decolonizing methodology, research always occurs within a contested terrain of meaning and the tension of competing ideas, in that colonizing power relations persist within contemporary institutions and society. Hence, decolonizing research is linked to emancipatory efforts to dismantle oppressive theories and practices, in an effort to transform existing conditions. This calls for a research process that can support the political creation of intellectual and social spaces where alternative readings of the world can exist in the interest of anticolonial practices that nourish our empowerment and liberation. Inherent to a counterhegemonic view of research is the creation of space for the ongoing development of our self-determination and the construction of yet unimagined ways of knowing and being in the world.

Alliance of theory and practice

Decolonizing interpretive research, as other forms of decolonizing methodologies, must be fundamentally linked to the practical intent of transforming inequities. Research then is informed by and exists in alliance with social practices. The emphasis here is in on what Freire (2012) terms *praxis*, where social relations are grounded in a reconstituting and self-generating process of reflection, dialogue, and action. Decolonizing interpretive research then must be understood as having purpose within the context of institutions and everyday life of the most affected or vulnerable populations (Dussel, 2003, 2013). Hence, critical research outcomes must always be linked to the real world; and as such, it must be flexible and fluid, able to shift and move according to the actual conditions that emerge within the context of human interactions. Similarly, research theory is always informed by practice, just as practice is always informed by the epistemological loyalties we embrace.

Conscientization

Decolonizing research seeks to support a purposeful and emancipatory interaction between the research and the people or the bodies of knowledge that are engaged in the course of study. Essential to this process is a deep concern for the development of voice, participation, and solidarity within the context of our communities, institutions, and larger society. Toward this end, knowledge construction of the research process is always understood as a collective process that engages the ongoing interactive process, shattering the subjective/objective binary so common to traditional notions of research. Through dialectical engagement, decolonizing research seeks to support knowing the world and self through a relational, communal, and democratizing process. At its core, there resides a deliberate intent to support the evolution of an anticolonial and decolonizing consciousness, where an expanding sense of our human interdependence is ever-present.[4] Wilson (2008), for example, speaks of the research of indigenous people as "a ceremony that allows us a raised level of consciousness and insight into our world" (p. 137). The ceremonial dimension in this approach is tied to the relational manner in which decolonizing interpretive researchers gather together consistently as a research community to break bread and participate in a shared and evolving processes of critique, questioning, verification, and affirmation. Similarly, the underlying outcome of decolonizing interpretive research is also linked to our ongoing commitment to subaltern communities and to the manner our labor can serve to support transformative social action on the ground.

These critical influences, in conjunction with the voices and sensibilities of indigenous and other subaltern researchers, push against the hegemonic epistemological tradition of the West, supporting the design and outcome of decolonizing interpretive studies based on rigorous decolonizing arguments that can move us toward an ethically liberating progression, while simultaneously shattering the boundaries of descriptive positivist notions of traditional research. As such, decolonizing interpretive studies must begin with a thoughtful and well-developed introduction that states the central problem and focus, in ways that reflect an anticolonial lens in the contextualization of the problem and the use of demographic data to illuminate the manner in which the coloniality of power has had concrete social and material consequences on subaltern populations. The introduction, therefore, provides readers with a glimpse into the conceptual frameworks most closely related to the phenomenon being studied, with an emphasis on dialectically situating the social or educational phenomenon within both historical and contemporary moments. This generally includes an engagement with the limitations of existing formulations, unexamined data, contradictory notions, the hidden curriculum of educational policies and practices (Apple, 2004), and other aspects that can support the critical theoretical interrogation and decolonizing analysis that will inform the discussions across the study.

All this, of course, signals a most grueling and precarious process, in the reformulation of existing hegemonic conceptualizations based on Western epistemologies of the subaltern, which must be systematically deconstructed by way of decolonizing epistemologies, ontologies, and the cultural wisdom brought to light by interrogations and analysis. It is from whence that the decolonizing interpretive researcher unfolds renewed emancipatory insights and new subaltern perspectives. These decolonizing perspectives, anchored to *a priori* knowledge of lived histories and non-Western epistemologies of the world, are exercised in the contestation, deconstruction, and reinvention of hegemonic practices within schools and subaltern communities. This also points to understanding that one's individual voice exists dialectically in relationship to a larger communal voice.

It is, however, important to not essentialize or reify the meaning of the critical influences discussed here, in that decolonizing researchers recognize that we are deeply accountable—or answerable, as Patel (2016) argues—for the exercise of our individual voices; voices complicated by the double consciousness of our positionality as researchers, who are forced to navigate daily the oppressed/oppressor dialectic of our subaltern existence. In that, as Savransky (2017) warns, the depth of our epistemological colonization "has not only infected conventional political and epistemological thinking in the West, but its critical versions as well" (p. 15). Yet, simultaneously, we are also keenly aware that our subaltern voices are intrinsically tied to the collective voices of our communities, historically subordinated by genocide, slavery, colonization, and imperialism to conserve the political and material interests of a domestic and internationalized economic apartheid.

Centering the subaltern voice

> You who understand the dehumanization of forced removal-relocation-reeducation-redefinition, the humiliation of having to falsify your own reality, your voice—you know. And often cannot say it. You try and keep on trying to unsay it, for if you don't, they will not fail to fill in the blanks on your behalf, and you will be said.
>
> *(Min-Ha, 2009)*

The politics of the subaltern voice engages forthrightly with the phenomenon of human oppression and its debilitating historical impact upon the identities, social location, representations, and material conditions of subaltern populations. Accordingly, our voices emerge from the tenacious and tireless navigation through the dehumanizing forces of silence and isolation, as Trinh Min-Ha (2009) suggests, in a quest to unsay and undo the distorted Eurocentric representations or historical settler portrayals placed upon indigenous and other subaltern populations (Patel, 2016). This notion calls forth the epistemicidal assertions of Boaventura de Sousa Santos (2005) and João Paraskeva (2011), which signals a phenomenon in which voices that emerge from knowledges outside the Western purview are not only rendered silent and invisible, but are often absorbed or destroyed, as is precisely the case with the *culture of forgetting* (Darder, 2014). This phenomenon is prompted by the colonizing epistemological influences of banking education, where researchers are expected to reject the complexities of native tongue and uncritically adopt the hegemonic language and cultural system imposed upon us by the dominant culture of institutional research. This further points to that repressive epistemological region that Santos (2007) calls the *abyssal divide*, where the voices of the Other are rendered irrelevant or non-existent.

It is also worth noting here that racializing class formations and implicit beliefs, attitudes, and values shaped by the impact of the abyssal divide persist in adherence to a *global coloniality of power* (Grosfoguel, 2011; Mignolo, 2011; Quijano, 2000) that further subjugates subaltern voices even within the geographic, academic, and political contexts of their original formation. As such, colonizing expectations of knowledge production continue to be defined by the ruling interests of the economically and politically powerful. In response, subaltern voices within the context of a decolonizing interpretive methodology call for a re-reading of history and the economy in ways that profoundly critique and challenge official scripts of colonization around the world and their postcolonial celebrations. By so doing, this methodology seeks to forthrightly expose the *colonial matrix of power* (Tlostanova & Mignolo, 2009)—which encompasses economic control, control of authority, control of the public sphere, and ideological control and legitimation of knowledge—forms of control that persists long after formal structures of colonial political rule cease (Patel, 2016; Wanderley & Faria, 2013; Smith, 1999). From this vantage point, our subaltern voices fueled by decolonizing interpretive sensibilities shed light on the whitewashed partiality and limitations of historically recorded accounts of knowledge, revealing the absence of subaltern voices that remain exiled and suppressed by the power of epistemicides (Paraskeva, 2011).

In direct contrast to traditional research, decolonizing research fiercely counters both Cartesian relativism and skepticism and Kantian transcendental reason, where "knowledge is either imperial or does not exist" (Alcoff, 2007, p. 88). Hence, subaltern voices often undertake oppositional interrogations of official claims that emerge from those sanctioned mainstream intellectuals who purport universal expertise in the production and navigation of explanatory knowledge *about* the lives and survival of those deemed as other—knowledge about which they themselves are tragically ungrounded and inexperienced. A central concern, of course, is the extent to which a colonizing or what Edward Said (1978) calls "orientalism" is implicated in the Western production of research expertise about the other and the perpetuation of an epistemic dynamic of othering. Here, the gaze that informs research analyzes bodies of knowledge with the explicit intent to sift and sort, emphasizing the differences between the West and the subaltern with the intention of preserving the privilege and supremacy of Western basic assumptions—which, as Chakrabarty (2000) notes, constitutes an essential dimension of colonial rule. Thus, an accompanying question is: to what extent do Western political and economic interests distort the perceptions of the other, where an underlying hidden curriculum is the assimilation of the other, in order to preserve the classed, racialized, gendered, abled, sexual, and religious hierarchies or supremacies of Western cultural domination around the globe?

Hence, it is not surprising that in mainstream accounts of history a "deep underlying assumption that emerges in [traditional] studies is the physical and mental laziness of 'non-Westerners' as an immanent quality that makes them unproductive" (Frenkel & Shenhav, 2003, p. 6). This view, often "substantiated" by scientific research that points to the inherent laziness and non-productivity of colonized savage barbarians (Rabinbach, 1991), has been reinforced by an all too common traditional research lens, steeped in notions of deficit, neutrality, individualism, and supremacy. Hence, colonizing research approaches have brutally undermined the social and material well-being of subaltern populations, often leaving our communities further exploited, disempowered, and excluded from participation in decision-making about our own lives and without access to the benefits or opportunities enjoyed by the wealthy and privileged. In response, subaltern voices brush fiercely across these oppressive interpretations in an effort to halt the assault, struggle to decolonize knowledge, and work to (re)produce knowledge forms that are in sync with the histories, cultures, languages, and cosmologies of the oppressed.

Nancy Fraser's (1990) concept of *Subaltern counterpublics* is useful here in that she speaks to the concept of "arenas where members of subordinate social groups invent and circulate counterdiscourses, which in turn permit them to formulate oppositional interpretations of their identities, interests, and needs" (p. 56). Herein is found the counterhegemonic dimension essential to decolonizing interpretive research; for without the "formulation of oppositional interpretations" or the itinerant and fluid attribute of subaltern voices, born of the deep dialectical tension between hegemonic and subaltern knowledges that must be courageously navigated, a genuinely decolonizing interpretive engagement would be impossible. It is for this reason that decolonizing interpretive analyses draw heavily on subaltern historical and cultural sensibilities.

Furthermore, decolonizing interpretive theorists draw on our own historical experiences, cultural knowledge, and the materiality of our collective conditions, as we seek to create the research agendas that are most in sync with and organic to our liberation. Of this Smith (1999) asserts, "while we should acknowledge there are multiple sites where the struggle against oppression and exploitation might be taken up, Indigenous peoples must set the agenda for change themselves, not simply react to an agenda that has been laid out for us by others" (p. 210). This is in line with Freire's (2012) insistence that the historical task of the oppressed is to liberate ourselves and Fanon's (1963) assertion that as colonized subjects liberate ourselves from the colonizing frameworks that have constricted our voices and consciousness, we "are all the time adding to [our] knowledge in the light of experience, [and] will come to show [ourselves] capable" (Fanon, 1963, p.141) of speaking the unspeakable and breaking with the culture of silence historically imposed upon our communities.

Further, Randeria (2007) argues:

> Sensitivity to the history of [these conditions] could be an important corrective to the presentism and Eurocentrism of most analyses ... with their propensity to overstate the singularity of the present and to posit a radical discontinuity between contemporary social life and the recent past.
>
> *(p 71)*

It is worth noting here that in the absence of this corrective, despite even conventional qualitative research efforts to expand positivist norms of scientific interrogation, the qualitative research arena still constitutes a colonizing or Eurocentric sphere of knowledge construction, dominated by an elite few. Consequently, despite research missions that advocate "social justice," *intellectual transgressions* unwittingly repress subaltern sensibilities and silence the knowledge and wisdom that can spring forth from our lived histories of colonization. About this Hall (2010) argues:

> The inability of Eurocentrists [researchers] to concede the colonial influence upon knowledge suggests their hegemony does not rise to the level of consciousness. Conversely, non-European [subaltern] groups are astutely aware of that influence. The result is a psychological colonization that has rendered knowledge all but totally irrelevant to ... confronting [issues of] non-European populations. Extended from psychological colonization is then unnecessary ignorance. Ignorance of [subaltern] populations is measured by the individual effort, which allows Eurocentrists to sustain themselves despite their intellectual transgressions.
>
> *(p. 18)*

These colonizing transgressions are carried out, as Said (1978) contends, "by making statements about it, authorizing views of it, describing it, by teaching it, settling it, ruling it: in short, [Western research has functioned as a hegemonic apparatus] for dominating, restructuring, and having authority over" (p. 3) subaltern knowledge production. In the process, the sensibilities and cultural insights offered by subaltern researchers are often met with irrational suspicions and hostile interrogations regarding the veracity and validity of not only the conclusions we posit, but also the very phenomenon, itself, we elect to examine through an interpretive approach—an approach generally conserved for the elite formation of settler philosophers, historians, and political scientists—in fields historically entrenched within an overwhelmingly Western, patriarchal, elitist, and deeply racializing interpretation of human existence.

In contrast, more recent decolonizing studies conducted by indigenous and subaltern researchers, such as Linda Tuhiwai Smith, Ngugi wa Thiong'o, Walter Mignolo, Sandy Grande, Achilles Mbembe, João Paraskeva, Eve Tuck, Wayne Yang, Leigh Patel, and others, whether explicitly stated to be so or not, illustrate powerful articulations of decolonizing the interpretive. Through bringing their subaltern voices and political sensibilities to the center of the discourse, the *epistemic disobedience* (Mignolo, 2000, 2013) that informs these studies has had a significant impact on the manner in which researchers in the field engage philosophically, historically, and qualitatively the lives of indigenous and other subaltern populations. I also want to note that, similarly, a decolonizing interpretive dynamic has been at work in many of the writings of subaltern scholars throughout the last century, including the writings of W. E. B. DuBois, Frantz Fanon, Aimé Césaire, Woodson G. Carter, Paulo Freire, Angela Davis, Chandra Tapalde Mohanty, Homi Bhabha, Vandana Shiva, Gilbert Gonzalez, Neville Alexander, Julius Nyerere, Gloria Anzaldúa, Grace Lee Boggs, Vine Deloria Jr., Audre Lorde, and bell hooks, to name a few, although this phenomenon has seldom been specifically articulated in the manner offered here.

Hence, more and more, we find subaltern sociologists, psychologists, political scientists, anthropologists, and literary writers from racialized, indigenous, and other subaltern communities that have labored to employ a decolonizing interpretive lens, in their efforts to extend and redefine our understanding of oppression and its impact on our lives and the lives of our peoples. Again, as members of subaltern communities, intimately grounded in the histories of oppression we interrogate and of which we write, the cultural and political sensibilities of subaltern voices offer key epistemological breakthroughs necessary to forging transformative political praxis out in the world, which might help to explain the resistance with which breakthroughs are often met within traditional research settings. This speaks, fundamentally, to the force of unsettling methodologies that create, legitimate, and answers to other ways of knowing, naming, and re-reading the world.

It is also telling that subaltern researchers have not always been aware of one another, since they have emerged within differing intellectual traditions and from a variety of historical contexts and geographical locations, where their lands and lives have been appropriated in the interest of colonial rule and capitalist accumulation. Yet, there seems, nonetheless, to be underlying similarities or recognizable sensibilities that emerge from the oppressor–oppressed dialectic (Freire, 2012) and constructing knowledge from the standpoint of our subaltern positionality. Views expressed in their writings also give credence to both Santos and Paraskeva's claims linked to the epistemological differences inherent to subaltern and indigenous sensibilities. This, of course, in no way implies that the subaltern voice exists as an essentialized, one-dimensional phenomenon—or as Spivak (cited in Wallace, 1999) asserts, "I do not think that just being in India is a union ticket to authenticity." Moreover, as Samek and Shultz (2017) argue, "[t]he long view of colonialism has taught us to be cautious when making universal claims given the brutal consequences for those who don't fit within the universal who could be subsequently de-humanized" (p. 38). However, what I suggest is that, despite the many differences at work in its expression, there is still indeed an *epistemological thread of subalternity* at work, which offers sufficient continuity to speak across conditions of oppression.

There is, however, a juncture here where the edges of a decolonizing interpretive methodology brush countercurrent to defensive retorts against the existence of any stability across subaltern voices beyond *strategic essentialism* (Spivak, 1988b). In contrast, the argument contends, without essentializing, that there exist decolonizing epistemological resonances that arise directly from our social location and collective experiences within the colonial matrix of power. About this Smith (1999) asserts:

> The talk about the colonial past is embedded in our political discourses, our humor, poetry, music, storytelling and an attitude about history. The lived experiences of imperialism and colonialism contribute another dimension to the ways in which terms like "imperialism" can be understood. This is a dimension that indigenous [and other subaltern] peoples know and understand well.
>
> *(p. 20)*

And it is, in fact, such resonances mitigated by our histories, political commitments, and community struggles that create possible spaces for dialogue and social transformation across our subaltern differences, as well as guide our decolonizing responses amid interactions with Western intellectuals that profess to be allied to the struggle for human liberation.

Decolonizing interpretive research then is uncompromisingly committed to creating counterhegemonic intellectual spaces in which new readings of the world can unfold, in ways that lead us toward possibilities of social and material change. Within the decolonial context of border thinking, new readings arise from enacting practices of delinking and epistemic disobedience—required if we are to express our difference and forge new ways of knowing and sensing the world (Mignolo, 2013). True to this underlying revolutionary aim, many subaltern researchers have drawn heavily from the transgressive traditions of anticolonial, decolonial and postcolonial writings to forge inroads into the contentious terrain of our intellectual borderlands. The dissident voices of subaltern researchers internationally have challenged the *epistemic violence* of Western academics. Through their interpretive praxis, they have confronted the underlying racialized and economic interests that surround academic research as commodity—generally constructed in the absence of subaltern sensibilities. In particular, Spivak takes to task even stalwart Western leftist theorists such as Foucault and Derrida, confronting the underlying economic interests and commodification that surround much of traditional research in the West.

Shattering neutral claims in Western representations of the subaltern suggests the need for decolonizing engagements that defy the hegemonic traditions of the Western interpretive lens. At the core of this critique is the incapacity of Westerners to listen or hear the Other, beyond enforcing and projecting their own Eurocentric or settler sensibilities upon us—rendering the indigenous and subaltern unseen and unheard. Hence, despite a variety of strident critiques issued over the years regarding, for example, Spivak's exceeding focus on epistemology and her retreat from political activism and the universal socialist project (Eagleton, 1999; Wallace, 1999), Spivak's willingness to risk stepping into "ways of thinking outside the European context that were discredited when capitalism became the most powerful imperialist force" (Spivak cited in Wallace, 1999) has offered subaltern researchers inspiration to explore and voice the particularities of our lived experiences; and, by so doing, unveil colonizing and crippling Western pronouncements of subaltern conditions that have shaped our lives—pronouncements that have generally failed to engage the persistent legacies of slavery, colonialization, and genocide in the world today. Moreover, sensitive to the ways in which colonialism has produced powerful stereotypes of the colonized, decolonizing researchers are apt to be far more attentive to the way others are characterised, aware that fixed definitions can produce distorting blind spots and result in a greater cost for indigenous people and other subaltern populations than for our mainstream counterparts.

Nevertheless, decolonizing intentions work to open the way for counter-hegemonic considerations that critically privilege the cultural histories and experiences of indigenous and other oppressed populations and further contribute to deconstructing and rethinking false and debilitating notions of subalternity. The autoethnographic episteme from whence subaltern research emanates, therefore, sits subtlety but powerfully beneath the colonizing epistemological structures—suggesting the emergence of decolonizing sensibilities at work in the findings, claims, and conclusions of indigenous and subaltern scholars from different parts of the world. Further, had indigenous and subaltern scholars not found the collective spiritual courage, physical wherewithal, psychological strength, and intellectual force to follow the inner stirrings of their subaltern voices and sensibilities, the decolonizing interpretive perspectives they have fashioned—centered on the lives of formerly colonized, enslaved, and genocided populations—would have remained ever silenced within the hegemonic abyssal divide of Western research traditions that have so often sought to reify and dispirit the very essence of our cultural existence, despite well-meaning assertions.

As such, decolonizing interpretive research speaks to oppositional and transformative studies that undertake a critical analysis of bodies of knowledge in any field related to the lives and survival of subaltern liberation. Moreover, it must be understood as inextricably situated in the values of decolonizing methodologies. Hence, were it not for the eloquent theoretical articulations of decolonizing methodologies by indigenous and subaltern researchers around the world, this work on decolonizing interpretive methodology would be devoid of the historical, political, and intellectual project that has nurtured its development. Nevertheless, most indigenous and subaltern researchers continue to experience the impact of colonization on our lives, "feeling the consequences of the eurocentric, scientifically driven epistemologies in which issues of power and voice are drowned by the powerful 'majority' players reflecting the 'master's' ideology" (Mutua & Swadener, 2004, p. ix). This to say, that the wounds and scars of coloniality persist in our lives and, as such, it necessitates our naming, "in relation to coloniality and its construction of the colonial difference" (Alcoff, 2007, p. 90).

Naming the politics of coloniality

> If we are to do anything about our individual and collective being today, then we have to coldly and consciously look at what imperialism has been doing to us and to our view of ourselves in the universe.
>
> *(Thiong'o, 1981)*

For more than 500 years the *coloniality of power* (Quijano, 2000) has been enacted through a fiercely imperialist project that has fiercely rejected and negated any rethinking of moral problems from the point of view of the most vulnerable populations (Dussel, 2003). Under its influence the doctrine of Manifest Destiny was conceived and practiced to the detriment of colonized and enslaved populations who were socially and economically exploited, enslaved, or genocided. One of the worst consequences of such a practice is the shameful creation of "economic dependency" among oppressed populations through what Fanon (1967) terms a "perverted logic." Hence, challenging the historical and contemporary impact of colonializing dependency—epistemologically and materially—is at the heart of decolonizing interpretive research, which aims to dismantle Western epistemicides (Mignolo, 2007; Paraskeva, 2011; Santos, 2007), reasserting history into our understanding of colonialism; that is, affirming the history and knowledge of indigenous and other subaltern populations negated by European modernity (Grande, 2004; Mignolo, 2000; Quijano, 2000).

Key to this analysis, then, is a decolonizing sensibility that recognizes the inseparability of coloniality with capitalist imperatives of European modernity. Colonialism, moreover, is understood

> as constitutive of modernity, of its teleological macro-narratives of human progress, and of the material base necessary to provide both the surplus and the self-representation required to imagine Europe as the vanguard of the human race. To put this another way, colonialism is constitutive of both the base and the superstructure of modernity.
>
> *(Alcoff, 2007, p. 85)*

Wanderley and Faria (2013) further argue:

> Contrary to the usual demarcation made by European modernity that sets its start in the seventeenth and eighteenth centuries, decolonial authors suggest

that modernity and coloniality have been initiated simultaneously when the Americas were "discovered" by Columbus in 1492 ... Since then, a colonial matrix of power (Mignolo, 2011) has been imposed and it lasts much after colonialism's political domination is ceased.

(pp. 4–5)

With this in mind, decolonizing interpretive research embodies a critical conceptual reading of history that profoundly critiques and challenges the dominance of European modernity and its corresponding epistemic coloniality (Ibarra-Colado, 2006; Mignolo, 2007; Grande, 2004), hence giving voice to suppressed knowledges from both North and South. As such, the episteme of modernity is, in fact, the colonial episteme embodied by the cultural hegemony of the West. According to Mignolo (2000, 2007, 2011), then, coloniality is the malevolent and inseparable side of modernity—a side that we cannot ignore in the struggle to decolonize knowledge and transform the social and material practices that shape subaltern life.

Naming the coloniality of power then points to explicitly engaging with the hegemonic apparatus at work in the distribution of epistemic, moral, and aesthetic resources that perpetuate the politics of empire (Quijano, 1998). Drawing on the writings of Wallerstein (1979), Mignolo (2000), Quijano (1991, 1993, 2000, 2007), Spivak (1988a), and Enloe (1990), Grosfoguel (2011) provides a useful list of hegemonic entanglements that define, structure, and epistemologically inform the European/capitalist/military/Christian/patriarchal/white/heterosexist/male globalized politics of coloniality:

1) a particular global class formation where a diversity of forms of labor (slavery, semi-serfdom, wage labor, petty-commodity production, etc.) co- exist and are organized by capital as a source of production of surplus value through the selling of commodities for a profit in the world market;

2) an international division of labor of core and periphery where capital organized labor in the periphery around coerced and authoritarian forms

3) an inter-state system of politico-military organizations controlled by European males and institutionalized in colonial administrations

4) a global racial/ethnic hierarchy that privileges European people over non-European people

5) a global gender hierarchy that privileges males over females and European Judeo-Christian patriarchy over other forms of gender relations

6) a sexual hierarchy that privileges heterosexuals over homosexuals and lesbians (it is important to remember that most indigenous peoples in the Americas did not consider sexuality among males a pathological behavior and had no homophobic ideology);

7) a spiritual hierarchy that privileges Christians over non-Christian/non-Western spiritualities institutionalized in the globalization of the Christian (Catholic and later, Protestant) church;

8) an epistemic hierarchy that privileges Western knowledge and cosmology over non-Western knowledge and cosmologies, and institutionalized in the global university system

9) a linguistic hierarchy between European languages and non-European languages that privileges communication and knowledge/theoretical production in the former and subalternize the latter as sole producers of folklore or culture but not of knowledge/theory

10) an aesthetic hierarchy of high art vs. naïve or primitive art where the West is considered superior high art and the non-West is considered as producers of inferior expressions of art institutionalized in Museums, Art Galleries and global art markets;

11) a pedagogical hierarchy where the Cartesian western forms of pedagogy are considered superior over non-Western concepts and practices of pedagogy;

12) a media/informational hierarchy where the West has the control over the means of global media production and information technology while the non-West do not have the means to make their points of view enter the global media networks;

13) an age hierarchy where the Western conception of productive life (ages between 15 and 65 years old) making disposable people above 65 years old is considered superior over non-Western forms of age classification, where the older the person, the more authority and respect he/she receives from the community;

14) an ecological hierarchy where the Western conceptions of "nature" (as an object that is a means towards an end) with its destruction of life (human and non- human) is privileged and considered superior over non-Western conceptions of the "ecology" which considers in its rationality the reproduction of life;

15) a spatial hierarchy that privileges the urban over the rural with the consequent destruction of rural communities, peasants and agrarian production at the world-scale.

Decolonizing interpretive researchers engage then the global coloniality of power as a way to comprehend the set of framing and organizing assumptions implicated in traditional forms of research that justify and substantiate hierarchies, while invisibilizing and silencing all that sits outside the purview of Western logic. More simply put, naming the politics of coloniality sheds light on colonial structures and the manner in which society obscures the pervasiveness of coloniality long after the removal of formal colonial rule (Patel, 2016). Furthermore, seeing the politics of coloniality "as paradoxical and self-serving logic helps to unsettle the terms on which settler colonialism is based and maintained." Explicitly naming the politics of coloniality also allows us to think through how the colonized were (and are) subjected not simply to a rapacious exploitation but also to a hegemonic system of Eurocentric knowledge, settler authority over all indigenous and subaltern resources, and a privileged "form of sociality, tied to a universalizing and totalizing ambition" (Venn, 2000, p. 19).

Fanon, however, reminds us that both the settler and the colonized came into existence by way of the politics of coloniality and, therefore, both are "the product of the colonial encounter" (Frenkel & Shenhav, 2003, p. 4). Within this construction, indigenous and other subaltern populations are categorized, classified, and ranked in ways that deem the colonized as less human than the European settlers who appropriated our lands. Patel (2016) notes "coloniality created savagery in order to claim domain over it and the lands of which the then-named savages were living" (p. 94). About this, Smith (1999) argues, "The principle of 'humanity' was one way in which the implicit or hidden rules could be shaped" (p. 27) and, thus, functioned to justify policies and practices of domestication, exploitation, and extermination. For example, Mignolo (2009) notes that racism "was the result of two conceptual inventions of imperial knowledge: that certain bodies were inferior to others, and that inferior bodies carried inferior intelligence" (pp. 19–20). It is not surprising then that "the struggle to assert and claim humanity has been a consistent thread of anti-colonial discourses on colonialism and oppression" (p. 27). However, it has not been without contradictions, particularly when our discourses of humanity have remained shackled to the oppressed/oppressor binary. Hence, a decolonizing view of humanity necessitates unsettling and shattering this binary by redefining our humanity across the multidimensional layers of our existences—existences shaped by the multiplicity of our histories, cultures, and lived experiences. This entails mobilizing a decolonizing interpretation of what it means to be human, which extends beyond imperialist commodification and simplistic colonizing negations that have falsely misconstrued the nature of our humanity.

Understanding and engaging the history of colonization from this critical vantage point sheds light on the whitewashed partiality and limitations of officially recorded accounts of history, revealing the absence of subaltern populations who remain exiled and suppressed by epistemicides (Paraskeva, 2011) that sustain the coloniality of power and its *abyssal divide*, where, as noted earlier, the other is rendered irrelevant or non-existent (Santos, 2007). Of this, Santos writes:

> What most fundamentally characterizes abyssal thinking is thus the impossibility of the co-presence of the two sides of the line. To the extent that it prevails, this side of the line only prevails by exhausting the field of relevant reality. Beyond it, there is only nonexistence, invisibility, non-dialectical absence.
>
> *(p. 1)*

However, "it is not enough to *acknowledge* the interpretive frame if that frame itself is not theorized in relation to coloniality and its construction" of what Mignolo calls the *colonial difference* (Alcoff, 2007, p. 90).

In our quest then to dissolve the closed boundaries of the coloniality of power, Mignolo suggest that we grapple with the concept of colonial difference, in an effort to unveil and displace the colonial logic employed historically to render subaltern populations as "other." Embedded in the colonial imagination that persists is a view of indigenous and other people of color as existing on the same historical trajectory and same aspirations as our settler counterparts, but simply primitive or less developed, whether biologically or culturally. In the process, actual human differences are invisibilized and made incomprehensible. Inherent to this decolonizing notion of colonial difference is the manner in which it can function to break us out of this simplistic logic of sameness, by exposing the manner in which power is implicated in the construction of difference—both ideologically and materially. In this way, we are able to decipher more readily the manner in which the coloniality of power produces, perpetuates, and manages the colonial difference in its quest for supremacy. Along the same vein, Mbembe (2015) argues that given the double character of decolonization—that is, the closure as well as possibility at work—the process must be grounded in a politics of difference.

At this juncture, it is worth noting the manner in which settler colonialism— where "a colonizing power exports indigenous peoples (as slaves or laborers), resources, knowledge, plants, metals, and/or animals to increase the wealth of the colonizer—as well as *internal colonialism*—violent management of an underclass of people and lands within the 'domestic' borders of the imperial nation via ghettos, reservations, borders, prisons, police, surveillance, and educational systems" (Bloom & Carnine, 2016)—persists in contemporary processes of colonization. Patel (2016) offers an example of this phenomenon in her critique of *deservingness*—long used within hegemonic societies to demarcate human worth and who justifiably deserves access to land resources, opportunities, power, and privilege. In a discussion of education and migration, Patel rightly asserts that "the ubiquity of deservingness demands a decolonial reckoning with the specifics of how it is deployed relative to differently racialized peoples in a settler society, how they are racially minoritized and majoritized, and fundamentally, how that creates connected yet distinct social locations, rights, and relationships to self, others, the state, and land" (p. 11). Moreover, this illustrates the ideological and epistemological underpinnings of the coloniality of power, which commonsensically creep into exclusionary practices related to meritocracy and evidenced-based research.

Therefore, the persistence of the *colonial matrix of power* (Mignolo, 2007; Patzi-Paco, 2004; Quijano, 2000)—"an organizing principle involving exploitation and domination exercised in multiple dimensions of social life" (Grosfoguel, 2011)—has been made possible through the deeply rooted hegemonic interplay of economic control, control of authority, control of the public sphere, and ideological control—in essence control of what knowledge is legitimated and what knowledge is excluded (Tlostanova & Mignolo, 2009). Through a complex manifestation of asymmetrical relations of power, cultural hegemony is solidified and perpetuated through the commonsense values, beliefs, and interests of the ruling class, and transmitted by way of the hidden curriculum of scientific research. In contrast, decolonizing interpretive researchers

are contesting at the level of knowledge, but we are also contesting a history of colonization and colonizing processes. If you understand schooling and education [as well as research] as "selection of knowledge" that is taught in institutions, and that dominant cultural groups can determine what knowledge is selected to be taught, then you will understand how schooling and education [and research] become sites for colonization and assimilation. The interests of the dominant white society at the university are able to be reproduced within the structures of social, political, and economic dominance, and so forth. In order to overcome Indigenous complicity in the reproduction of white social, economic, and political privilege, [decolonizing researchers] need a philosophy that allows us to engage within the academy, within the ambit of what I call "the politics of truth."

(Kovach, 2009, p. 29)

Through rupturing the logic of Western epistemicides, we can begin to build a collective path toward unraveling colonizing forms of knowledge and, by so doing keep our studies from becoming inadvertently ensnared by colonizing assumptions. However, this decolonizing process does not mean we move completely into a different space, but rather that we are committed to the transformation "of the rigidity of epistemic and territorial *frontiers* established and controlled by the coloniality of power" (Mignolo, 2000, p. 12). Moreover, it is worth noting that "the fact that one is socially located in the oppressed side of power relations does not automatically mean that he/she is epistemologically thinking from a subaltern location" (Grosfoguel, 2011, p. 5), given the success of hegemony in shrouding the dynamics and structure of oppression in contemporary societies. In responding to this complexity, various decolonizing scholars, including Mignolo, Dussel, and Anzaldúa, have turned to the emancipatory notion of *border thinking*, which aims toward the dissolution and transformation of rigid epistemological borders, in ways that profoundly call into question colonizing conceptualizations of humanity. As might be obvious, "the goal of border thinking is de-subalternizing knowledge itself" (Alcoff, 2007, p. 94), in ways that create ample creative spaces for demythologizing, disrupting, and re-reading our lives and the world in transformative ways.

Demythologizing, disrupting, and re-reading

[Colonizing versions of research] must be recalled and de-commissioned if we have to put history to rest, free ourselves from our own entrapment in [its] mythologies and open a future for all here and now.

(Mbembe, 2015)

Beyond the critical influences discussed earlier, centering the subaltern voice and naming the coloniality of power are considered major tenets at work in decolonizing methodologies. Alongside these two important principles, decolonizing interpretive scholars engage with processes of inquiry that support the demythologizing of hegemonic beliefs, disrupt colonial epistemological structures of knowledge formation, and offer emancipatory re-readings of colonizing notions of human existence. Savransky (2017) speaks of this as the cultivation of a new form of realism … that takes the risk of asserting the reality of what is deemed improbable, implausible, marginalized, suppressed, irrelevant, even scandalous, and seeks to draw out its possible implications for the transformation of what is considered credible, reliable and serious.

(p. 22)

It is precisely through such a process that the *demythologizing of hegemonic beliefs* can be actualized. Mbembe (2015) argues that a myth is "the most corrosive and the most lethal when it makes us believe that it is everywhere; that everything originates from it and it has no outside" (p. 3). Hence, shattering oppressive myths that profoundly litter the commonsensical imagination go hand in hand with the aims of decolonizing interpretive research, which seeks to promote and sustain the self-determination of indigenous and subaltern communities. Grosfoguel (2011) reminds us that this is particularly significant, given the manner in which Western epistemologies conveniently delink

ethnic/racial/gender/sexual epistemic location from the subject that speaks [or researches] … producing a myth about a Truthful universal knowledge that covers up, that is, conceals who is speaking as well as the geo-political and body-political epistemic location in the structures of colonial power/knowledge from which the subject speaks.

(p. 6)

A variety of myths have perpetuated legacies of colonization and have been particularly destructive to the lives of indigenous and subaltern populations. When oppressive myths become ensconced and gain currency within the public sphere, they have very real impact on intuitional policies and practices across societal institutions, often promoting assimilative protocols and expectations that further betray the cultural sovereignty of indigenous and subaltern populations. One such myth is that of the professional expert. This refers to the privileged positionality extended to those who are seen as being unsituated, neutral, and objective. In other words, the belief that dispassionate and disinterested figures, "trained" by universities or professional programs, are far more equipped to define, speak, and resolve objectively the difficulties and suffering at work in the lives of the oppressed. In direct opposition to the myth that individuals exist as non-situated egos, Haraway (1988) asserts that all knowledge is situated and bound by the epistemological traditions that inform its production. Moreover, Patel (2016) reminds us that the exercise of the freewheeling myth of external expert as change agent, so prevalent across settler societies and the research arena, in particular, functions "as [a colonizing] arm of state-sanctioned positioning of intellect" (p. 44), which extends as a mechanism of social control. Other myths that similarly abound in the West include the privileging of whiteness, rugged individualism, universalism, and the survival of the fittest—emerging and perpetuated by enduring entanglements of colonialism within the context of globalized capital and settler appropriations.

The political sensibilities from whence decolonizing interpretive research emerges are highly complex, diverse, and uncompromisingly *disruptive of hegemonic epistemologies* fixed by schemes of patriarchal dominance, class divisions, heterosexism, abled bodies, and racializing reproduction. Targeted here, in particular, is the universalizing epistemological paradigm—a colonizing paradigm of empirical inquiry anchored in elite practices of patriarchal dominance, class divisions, linguistic genocide, heterosexism, abled bodies, and institutional structures deeply mired by racism and class oppression—enacted through an exclusionary discourse of institutional fit or scientific validity. Of this Fanon (1963) argues,

> Colonization is not satisfied merely with holding a people in its grips and emptying the native's brain of all form and content. By a kind of perverted logic, it turns to the past of the oppressed people, and distorts, disfigures and destroys it.
>
> *(p. 210)*

Accordingly, epistemologies that embolden the supremacy of Western research approaches often result in the social and material subordination of subaltern knowledge and wisdom, deemed suspect and a threat to the veracity of so-called objective claims. For example, allegiance persists to an epistemologically closed scientific method, informed by a predilection to conquest and a decontextualized and detemporalized method of sifting, sorting, and measuring that is said to produce "evidenced-based" knowledge that is universal and "can be applied anywhere and anytime" (Battiste, 2013). In its wake, a propensity for reductive thinking and objective measurement prevails within traditional research, which has systematically hijacked communal and intuitive ways of knowing, by converting human phenomenon into universalized numerical standards that both conflate and sever knowledge from context. Mbembe (2015) argues,

> [t]his hegemonic notion of knowledge production has generated discursive scientific practice and has set up interpretive frames that make it difficult to think outside these frames. But this is not all ... [i]t also actively represses anything that actually is articulated, thought and envisioned from outside of these frames.
>
> *(p. 10)*

In direct contrast, decolonizing approaches to research decenter Western-based notions of scientific neutrality, reliability, and validity, by advancing an evolving and itinerant epistemology—that is, an organic, fluid, and flexible means of knowing the world that, according to Paraskeva (2011), destabilizes fixed knowledge depictions and absolute beliefs of our time. This entails a rupturing of Western epistemologies rooted in abstract formulations devoid of both the internal and external negotiations that shape subaltern life, particularly with respect to the most impoverished. This rupturing is an absolute necessary step in that all knowledge is not only not equal, but has had serious consequences for indigenous and subaltern populations. Instead, knowledge must be understood as situated within both place and time, in that there is not an automatic transferability (Patel, 2016, p. 61). *Subaltern reason* supports us here to "rethink and reconceptualize the stories that have been told and the conceptualization that has been put into place to divide the world between Christians and pagans, civilized and barbarians, modern and pre-modern, and developed and undeveloped regions ad people" (Mignolo, 2000, p. 98).

The systematic disruption of hegemonic epistemologies offers us then fertile ground from which to foster non-abyssal thinking and knowledge (Savransky, 2017), in our efforts to posit liberatory epistemological and ontological critiques, in ways that support our redefinition and transformation of dominant readings of subalternity. Grounded in our political struggles for self-determination, decolonizing interpretive researchers must nevertheless also grapple with the dissonance of our own transgressive epistemological sensibilities, so that we can collectively work to disrupt the epistemological drive to conquer embedded in the Eurocentric imagination. As such, subaltern interpretive research emerges through a courageous and yet risky, itinerant inquiry process that brushes hegemonic beliefs of culture, knowing, and society against our non-Western epistemological sensibilities—transgressive sensibilities that seek to unfold life beyond the persistent grip of the coloniality of power. Drawing from Santos, Savransky (2017) notes that this demands first a critical interrogation of Western values upon which traditional research is founded; and second, reclaiming old or hidden knowledges, while developing new ways of knowing that intimately connect us to our study, rather than alienating us and relegating us to impartial and distanced observers. Toward this aim, decolonizing interpretive research also seeks to create the epistemological conditions that permit us to "capture the immense variety of critical discourses and practices and to valorize and maximize their transformative potential … [through] conditions that demand an *epistemological reconstruction*" (Santos, 2014, p. 42).

It is precisely through this process of epistemological reconstruction that we establish possibilities for *emancipatory re-reading*. Hence, it is not incidental that decolonizing interpretive researchers, who have worked to demythologize hegemonic beliefs and moved toward epistemological disruptions, also seek opportunities to participate in emancipatory re-readings of practices, texts, relationships, language, and structures that impact the lives of indigenous and subaltern populations. More often than not, we arrive to such conclusions and theories anchored, as discussed earlier, to a decolonizing sensibility of subaltern existence—that is, our re-reading is often reflective of communal border knowledges, which have emerged from our lifelong struggles to navigate across epistemological tensions associated with our cultural, social, political, spiritual, and academic survival as border intellectuals (Darder, 2011). This also reflects what DuBois (1903) terms *double consciousness*, Fanon (1967) calls *twoness*, Zea (1988) refers to as *double reality*, and I call *bicultural* (Darder, 2012) in my earlier work on culture and power—all subaltern scholars writing about the particularities of the development of consciousness within the context of our subalternity. More importantly, this subaltern quality of double positionality is considered key to what Alcoff (2007) refers to as our *border's epistemic resources*.

Similarly, our navigation of the difficult epistemological tensions of our subaltern positionality has also shaped us as radical makers of meaning and communal social actors who have elected, painstakingly so, to ground our research within an anticolonial episteme that permits us "to think from both traditions and, at the same time, from neither of them" (Mignolo, 2000, p. 67). As such, the underlying ethos of our efforts to participate in the emancipatory re-reading of our world is also grounded in an unquestionable epistemological shift in the production of knowledge. In so doing, we have also labored together to offer more just and emancipatory political readings of our world, within both the academic borderlands and our everyday struggles for liberation. From this vantage point, we concur with Tuck and Yang (2012), "decolonization is not a metaphor," rather it embodies a purpose to unsettle hegemonic theories, policies, and practices, to disrupt settler colonialism, to recover stolen lands, and to support concrete forms of transformation to the social and material suffering experienced within our communities.

A decolonizing ethical stance

> Nobody in the World, nobody in history, has ever gotten their freedom by appealing to the moral sense of the people who were oppressing them.
>
> *(Shakur, 1987)*

Through our evolving capacity to labor alongside decolonizing principles of research, decolonizing interpretive researchers mobilize through our writings an ethics of liberation deeply founded on a politics of difference, solidarity, a fluid and organic understanding of humanity, and an ever-present moral responsibility for transforming our own lives and our communities. Beyond epistemological concerns then is also an endeavor to communicate a decolonizing ethical stance through our voices and participation in the larger political project of liberation. There is, then, a significant dimension at work here, in that it is precisely from what bell hooks (1994) calls the "authority of lived experience"—generally rendered marginal and irrelevant to mainstream research—that indigenous and subaltern voices find the veracity to speak, to question, to transgress, and to reinvent the distorting moral discourses of the powerful, along with conditions of material and social inequality that have perpetuated political and economic destruction in our communities. Accordingly, positionality and context matter deeply when we contemplate questions of ethics, particularly within the context of decolonizing research. About this, Smith (1999) reminds us, "When indigenous people become the researchers and not merely the researched, the activity of research is transformed. Questions are framed differently, priorities are ranked differently, problems are defined differently, and people participate on different terms" (p. 193). Moreover, Fals-Borda (2006) argues, "It is preferable for us to seek our own explanations for building an alternative paradigm, by studying our indigenous or founding regional groups and emphasizing their values of human solidarity" (cited in Zavala, 2013, p. 58).

In concert with this radical conceptualization of decolonizing interpretive research are relational processes of social inquiry, critique, and cultural reformulation (or reinvention, as Freire would say) that strike at the very heart of dominant ideologies of individualism, linked to colonizing moral perspectives that reinscribe oppressive social formations and sustain recalcitrant inequalities, intractable social exclusions, and the alienating disaffiliation of subalternity. This, as Patel (2016) correctly reminds us, is never a simple undertaking, given centuries of colonial structuring and the colonial logic of conquest that persists. A decolonizing interpretive process must entail then a multitude of careful (re-)readings of the world and of subaltern histories, in ways that critically undo coloniality and openly challenge what Freire (2012) referred to as the *tragic dilemma of the oppressed*. More importantly, subaltern ethical relationships in the world, as they emerge between the subject and object or signifier and signified, must be understood as situated and mediated within the social and material conditions of contemporary capitalist production. As such, colonizing notions of subalternity rooted in assimilative official transcripts of society and generally governed by the interests of the wealthy and powerful are targeted for dismantling. Toward this end, decolonizing interpretive researchers labor under a set of ethical considerations of difference,

> fundamentally mediated by power relations that are socially and historically constituted; that facts can never be isolated from the domain of values or removed from some form of ideological inscription; that the relationship between concept and object and between signifier and signified is never stable or fixed and is often mediated by the social relations of capitalist production and consumption; that language is central to the formation of subjectivity (conscious and unconscious awareness); that certain groups in any society and particular societies are privileged over others and, although the reasons for this privileging may vary widely, the oppression that characterizes contemporary societies is most forcefully reproduced when subordinates accept their social status as natural, necessary, or inevitable; that oppression has many faces and that focusing on only one at the expense of others (e.g., class oppression versus racism) often elides the interconnections among them; and, finally, that mainstream research practices are generally, although most often unwittingly, implicated in the reproduction of systems of class, race, and gender oppression.
>
> (*Kincheloe & McLaren, 2005*)

Furthermore, the intentionality of interpretive research is grounded in what Dussel (2013) called an *ethics of liberation,* which encompasses a rethinking of the totality of moral problems from the point of view of the most oppressed. This ethical concern within decolonizing interpretive research mobilizes us to (re)define and (re)articulate absences and emergences of knowledge claims from our subalternity, in order to set forth deco- lonizing strategies of engagement for altering current hegemonic discourses and practices in the world, which perpetuate colonizing and economically impoverishing aberrations. From this vantage point, Santos (2014) points to imagining, simultaneously, the end of capitalism and the end of colonialism, in ways that unambiguously situate our knowledges within history and unsettle imperial claims to both epistemic supremacy and material domination over the world, its resources, and its peoples.

However, given "the praxis of decolonization is not without contradictions" (Zavala, 2013, p. 57), Santos' critique also extends to the realm of critical theory, where anticolonial perspectives can still inadvertently reinscribe the settler logic of coloniality, particularly with respect to claims tied to "the repatriation of indigenous land and life" (Tuck & Yang, 2012, p. 1). With similar concerns in mind, Dussel (2003, 2013) proposes an *analectic view* (as opposed to dialectic) in his decolonizing ethics of liberation, which more expansively stretches the terrain of cognitive justice in making meaning of the world, giving greater significance to ontological and cosmological dimensions usually relegated to the waste bin of humanity. More specifically, an analectic perspective: (1) embraces alterity (i.e., social class, ethnicity, generation, gender, ability, sexuality, etc.) in our interrogations of the world, which rather than focusing on the negation, seeks to construct knowledge from the multiplicity and multidimensionality that exists outside of the totality of the dominant system of thought; (2) engages with a social realist ontology (which Dussel sees as more the question akin to liberation), which provides for understanding and engaging ourselves beyond simply the legacy of our colonization; and (3) in its dissolution of individualism, echoes Marx, by taking seriously the idea of our human essence as the ensemble of social relations; that is, we are created in and through social relations and thus, society is part of us, as much as we are a part of society (Burton, 2013).[5]

Indigenous and subaltern researchers who seek to embark upon an analectically inspired approach—or what Santos (2014) calls *postabyssal thought*—must not be only ethically committed to reinterpreting the world, but also to insurgently cultivating an *ecology of knowledges* (Santos, 2014) for the embodied remaking of the current social and material conditions that sustain our subalternity. Inherent here is a dynamic reorientation toward a reality of knowledge production informed by an ethics of liberation and the radicalization of consciousness—a revolutionary process, anchored within our histories of survival and the contingencies of everyday life (Darder, 2015). Therefore, there is no illusive ethical claim of neutrality or objectivity here, in that a fundamental purpose and aim of decolonizing interpretive research is to nurture, epistemologically and ontologically, liberatory articulations, as well as transformative participations in the larger political project for our liberation.

With all this in mind, decolonizing interpretive research articulates an ethical understanding of liberation that supports options for political shifts in how we comprehend difference and our place in the world with respect to others. This suggests new ways in which we "answer to a different set of ethical coordinates than settler colonialism" (Patel, 2016, p. 73). In terms of this notion of *answerability*, Patel (2016) calls us to be ethically responsible, accountable, and part of ongoing exchange related to learning, to knowledge, and to context. Of this she writes,

"Answerability means that we have responsibilities as speakers, listeners, and those responsibilities include stewardship of ideas and learning, ownership" (p. 74). Spivak similarly "invites [us] to look at [our] own context, positioning and complicities, to unlearn [our] privilege, to establish an ethical relationship to difference and to learn to learn from below" (Andreotti, 2007, p. 69). Inherently, these ideas signal a decolonizing ethics of difference that centers the subaltern voice as responsibly communal, demythologizes commonsensical notions of a detached ethics, situates knowledge production, exposes the coloniality of power, disrupts Eurocentric epistemicides, and provides itinerant re-readings of historical, political, conceptual, and everyday life.

As a revolutionary praxis, the restoration of our communal humanity is privileged within decolonizing interpretive research, where the subaltern researcher engages systematically in a critical process of problem-posing (Freire, 2012), so as to reformulate truths that are in line with our political self-determination. It is precisely though a rigorous and sustained progression of problematization that subaltern interpretive researchers arrive to decolonizing conclusions—conclusions that reassert formally negated histories, cultural knowledge, and lived experiences as legitimate and sustaining dimensions of both knowledge construction and contemporary reality, despite our legacies of social and material subordination. Through this process, decolonizing interpretive research is fueled by a radical humanizing political commitment to recover/uncover—through our ongoing interrogation of the oppressive structural forces that shape our lives—the knowledge indispensable to a culturally democratic and economically just future. By so doing, decolonizing interpretive research offers powerful renditions of liberated voices that bravely posit anticolonial, anti-capitalist, and anti-racist directions for social change, through a decolonizing praxis of ethical human inquiry, sovereign communal relationships of love and solidarity, and our unbending commitment to the freedom to be.

Notes

1 See the historical discussion of critical pedagogy in the introduction to the *Critical Pedagogy Reader* (Darder et al., 2017).
2 This discussion of the principles of critical research is based on the introduction to the *Critical Pedagogy Reader* (Darder et al., 2017), where critical pedagogical principles are defined.
3 In the last section of this chapter, I briefly discussion Dussel's analectical view of knowledge, which pushes against critical conceptualizations of the dialectic in ways that transform epistemological possibilities for cognitive justice, within the context of his discussion of an ethics of liberation.
4 See chapter three on "conscientização" in *Freire & Education* (Darder, 2015).
5 Given my own academic preparation and intellectual history as a colonized subject of the United States, my work over the years, including this book, draws more heavily on the critical tradition, despite ways in which my thinking intersects with Dussel's notion of analectic thought. However, I suspect as I continue to engage, interrogate, and rethink the politics of decolonization in my future research, this analectic view of knowledge will become more apparent in my articulation.

References

Alcoff, L. M. (2007). Mignolo's epistemology of coloniality. *CR: The New Centennial Review* 7(3), 79–101.

Andreotti, V. (2007). An ethical engagement with the other: Spivak's ideas in education. *Critical Literacy: Theories and Practices* 1(1), 69–79.

Apple, M. (2004). *Ideology & curriculum*. New York: Routledge.

Battiste, M. (2013). *Decolonizing education: Nourishing the learning spirit*. Saskatoon, Canada: Purich Publishing.

Bauman, Z. (1995). *Life in fragments*. New York: Blackwell.

Bloom, L. M., & Carnine, B. (2016). Towards decolonization and settler responsibility: Reflections on a decade of indigenous solidarity organizing. CounterPunch. Retrieved from www.counterpunch.org/2016/10/03/towards-decolonization-and-settler-responsibi lity-reflections-on-a-decade-of-indigenous-solidarity-organizing/.

Burton, M. H. (2013). The analectic turn: Critical psychology and the new political context. *Les cahiers psychologie politique* 23. Retrieved from http://lodel.irevues.inist.fr/cahiersp sychologiepolitique /index.php?id=2465.

Carlson, D. L., & Apple, M. (1998). *Power/knowledge/pedagogy: The meaning of democratic education in unsettling times*. Boulder: Westview.

Chakrabarty, D. (2000). *Provincializing Europe: Postcolonial thought and historical difference*. Princeton: Princeton University Press.

Darder, A. (2011). *A dissident voice: Essays on culture, pedagogy, and power*. New York: Peter Lang.

Darder, A. (2012 [1991]). *Cultural and power in the classroom* (2nd edition). Boulder: Paradigm.

Darder, A. (2014). Cultural hegemony, language, and the culture of forgetting: Interrogating restrictive language policies. In P. Orelus (Ed.), *Affirming language diversity in schools and society: Beyond linguistic apartheid*. New York: Routledge. 35–53.

Darder, A. (2015). *Freire and education*. New York: Routledge.

Darder, A., Baltodano, M., & Torres, R. D. (2017). *Critical pedagogy reader*. New York: Routledge.

DuBois, W. E. B. (1903). *The souls of black folk*. Chicago: A. C. McClurg.

Dussel, E. (2003). An ethics of liberation: Fundamental hypotheses. *Concilium* 172, 54–63.

Dussel, E. (2013). *Ethics of liberation: In the age of globalization and exclusion*. Durham, NC: Duke University Press.

Eagleton, T. (1999). In the gaudy supermarket. *London Review of Books* 21(10), 3–6.

Enloe, C. (1990). *Bananas, beaches and bases: Making feminist sense of international politics* (1st edition). Berkeley: University of California Press.

Fals-Borda, O. (2006). The north-south convergence: A 30-year first person assessment of PAR. *Action Research* 4(3), 351–358.

Fanon, F. (1963). *The wretched of the earth*. New York: Grove Press.

Fanon, F. (1967). *Black skins, white masks*. New York: Grove Press.

Fraser, N. (1990). Rethinking the public sphere: A contribution to the critique of actually existing democracy. *Social Text* 26/26, 56–80.

Freire, P. (1998). *Pedagogy of freedom*. New York: Continuum.

Freire, P. (2012 [1970]). *Pedagogy of the oppressed*. New York: Seabury.

Frenkel, M. & Shenhav, Y. (2003). *Decolonizing organization theory: Between orientalism and occidentalism*. Retrieved from www.mngt.waikato.ac.nz/ejrot/cmsconference/2003/procee dings/postcolonial/Frenkel.pdf.

Giroux, H. (1981). *Ideology, culture, and the process of schooling.* Philadelphia: Temple University Press.

Giroux, H. (1983). *Theory & resistance.* Westport: Bergin & Garvey.

Gramsci, A. (1971). *Selections from prison notebooks.* New York: International Publications.

Grande, S. (2004). *Red pedagogy: Native American social and political thought.* New York: Rowman & Littlefield.

Grosfoguel, R. (2011). Decolonizing post-colonial studies and paradigms of political economy. *Transmodernity* 1(1), 1–37. Retrieved from http://escholarship.org/uc/item/21k6t3fq.

Hall, R. E. (2010). *An historical analysis of skin color discrimination in America: Victimism among victim group populations.* New York: Springer.

Haraway, D. (1988). Situated knowledges: The science question in feminism and the privilege of partial perspective. *Feminist Studies* 14(1988): 575–599.

hooks, b. (1994). *Teaching to transgress.* New York: Routledge.

Ibarra-Colado, E. (2006). Organization studies and epistemic coloniality in Latin America: Thinking otherness from the margins. *Organization* 13: 463–488.

Kahn, R. (2010). *Critical pedagogy, ecoliteracy, & planetary crisis.* New York: Peter Lang.

Kellner, D. (1995). *Media culture: Cultural studies, identity, and politics between the modern and the postmodern.* New York: Routledge.

Kincheloe, J. (2008). *Knowledge and critical pedagogy.* New York: Springer.

Kincheloe, J. L., & McLaren, P. (2005). Rethinking critical theory and qualitative research. In N. Denzin & Y. Lincoln (Eds.), *The SAGE handbook of qualitative research* (3rd edition). Thousand Oaks: SAGE Publications. 303–342.

Kincheloe, J., McLaren, P., Steinberg, S., & Monzo, L. (2017). Critical pedagogy and qualitative research: Advancing the bricolage. In N. Denzin & Y. Lincoln (Eds.), *The SAGE handbook of qualitative research.* Thousand Oaks: SAGE Publications. 241–259.

Kovach, M. (2009). *Indigenous methodologies: Characteristics, conversations, and contexts.* Toronto: University of Toronto Press

Mbembe, A. (2015). Decolonizing knowledge and the question of the archive. Lecture delivered at University of the Witwatersrand, June 9. Retrieved from https://wiser.wits.ac.za/system/files/Achille %20Mbembe%20-%20Decolonizing%20Knowledge%20and%20the%20Question%20of%20the%20Archive.pdf.

McLaren, P. (1986). *Schooling as a ritual performance.* New York: Routledge.

Mignolo, W. (2000). *Local histories/global designs: Coloniality, subaltern knowledges, and border thinking.* Princeton: Princeton University Press.

Mignolo, W. (2007). Delinking: The rhetoric of modernity, the logic of coloniality and the grammar of de-coloniality. *Cultural Studies* 21(2–3), 449–514.

Mignolo, W. (2009). Independent thought and colonial freedom. *Theory, Culture & Society* 26(7–8), 1–23.

Mignolo, W. (2011). *The darker side of western modernity: Global futures, decolonial options.* London: Duke University Press.

Mignolo, W. (2013). Geopolitics of sensing and knowing: On {de}coloniality, border thinking, and epistemic disobedience. *Confero* 1(1), 129–150.

Min-Ha, T. T. (2009). *Women, native, other.* Bloomington: Indiana University Press.

Mutua, K., & Swadener, B. B. (2004). *Decolonizing research in cross-cultural contexts: Critical personal narratives.* Albany: State University of New York Press.

Paraskeva, J. (2011). *Conflicts in curriculum theory.* New York: Palgrave.

Patel, L. (2016). *Decolonizing educational research: From ownership to answerability.* New York: Routledge.

Patzi-Paco, Felix (2004). *Sistema comunal. Una propuesta alternativa al sistema liberal*. La Paz: Comunidad de Estudios Alternativos.

Quijano, A. (1991). Colonialidad y modernidad/racionalidad. *Perú indígena* 29, 11–20.

Quijano, A. (1993). "Raza", "Etnia" y "Nación" en Mariátegui: Cuestiones Abiertas. Roland Forgues (Ed.), *José Carlos Mariátegui y Europa: El Otro Aspecto del Descubrimiento*. Lima: Empresa Editora Amauta S.A. 167–187.

Quijano, A. (1998). La colonialidad del poder y la experiencia cultural latinoamericana. Roberto Briceño-León & Heinz R. Sonntag (Eds.), *Pueblo, época y desarrollo: la sociología de América Latina*. Caracas: Nueva Sociedad. 139–155.

Quijano, A. (2000). Coloniality of power, Eurocentrism, and Latin America. *Napantla: Views from the South* 1(3), 533–580.

Quijano, A. (2007). Coloniality and modernity/rationality. *Cultural Studies* 21(2–3), 168–178.

Rabinbach, A. (1991). *The human motor: Energy, fatigue and the origins of modernity*. New York: Basic Books.

Randeria, S. (2007). Legal pluralism, social movements and the post-colonial state in India: Fractured sovereignty and differential citizenship. In B. de Sousa Santos. *Another knowledge is possible: Beyond northern epistemologies*. London, UK: Verso. 41–74.

Rudestam, E., & Newton, R. R. (2007). *Surviving your dissertation*. Thousand Oaks: Sage Publications.

Said, E. (1978). *Orientalism*. New York: Vintage Books.

Samek, T., & Shultz, L. (2017). *Information ethics, globalization and citizenship*. Jefferson: McFarland.

Santos, B. de Sousa (2005). *Democratizing democracy: Beyond the liberal democratic canon*. London: Verso.

Santos, B. de Sousa (2007). *Another world is possible: Beyond northern epistemologies*. London: Verso.

Santos, B. de Sousa (2014). *Epistemologies of the south: Justice against epistemicide*. Boulder: Paradigm Publishers.

Savransky, M. (2017). A decolonial imagination: Sociology, anthropology and the politics of reality. *Sociology* 5(1), 11–26.

Shakur, A. (1987). *Assata: An autobiography*. London: Zed Books.

Shor, I. (1987). *A pedagogy for liberation: Dialogues on transforming education*. Santa Barbara and Westport: Bergin & Garvey.

Smith, L. T. (1999). *Decolonizing methodologies*. London: Zed Books.

Spivak, G. C. (1988a). Can the subaltern speak? In C. Nelson & L. Grossberg (Eds.), *Marxism and the interpretation of culture*. Urbana: University of Illinois Press. 271–316.

Spivak, G. C. (1988b). Subaltern studies: Deconstructing historiography. In *In other worlds: Essays in cultural politics*. New York: Routledge. 197–221.

Thiong'o, N. wa (1981). *Decolonizing the mind*. London: James Currey Ltd.

Tlostanova, M. V., & Mignolo, W. (2009). Global coloniality and the decolonial option. *Kult 6: Special Issue on Epistemologies of Transformation*. Department of Culture and Identity. Roskilde University. 130–147. Retrieved from http://postkolonial.dk/artikler/kult_6/MIGNOLO-TLOSTANOVA.pdf.

Tuck, E., & Yang, K. W. (2012). Decolonization is not a metaphor. *Decolonization: Indigeneity, Education, & Society* 1(1), 1–40.

Venn, C. (2000). *Occidentalism: Modernity and subjectivity*. London: Sage.

Wallace, J. (1999). Deconstructing Gayatri. *The Times Higher Education*, July 30. Retrieved from www.timeshighereducation.com/features/deconstructing-gayatri/147373.article.

Wallerstein, I. (1979). *The capitalist world-economy*. Cambridge: Cambridge University Press.

Wanderley, S., & Faria, A. (2013). Border thinking as historical decolonial method: Reframing dependence studies to (re)connect management and development. EnANPAD. Retrieved from www.anpad.org.br/admin/pdf/2013_EnANPAD_EOR2021.pdf.

Wilson, S. (2008). *Research is ceremony: Indigenous research methods*. Winnipeg: Fernwood Publishing.

Zavala, M. (2013). What do we mean by decolonizing research strategies? *Decolonization: Indigeneity, Education, & Society* 2(1), 55–71.

Zea, L. (1988). Identity: A Latin American philosophical problem. *e Philosophical Forum* XX (1–2), 33–42.

PART II
Decolonizing principles

Once upon a time, scholars assumed that the knowing subject in the disciplines is transparent, disincorporated from the known and untouched by the geo-political configuration of the world in which people are racially ranked are racially configured ... Today that assumption is no longer tenable.[1]

---

1   Walter Mignolo, Independent thought and colonial freedom, *Theory, Culture & Society* 15 (7–8), p. 1.

2

CENTERING THE SUBALTERN VOICE[1]

Kortney Hernandez

Through every experience and expression of my life, a deep spiritual process has connected my being and my knowing with the suffering and struggle of others, as I have attempted in community to make sense of a world that was not constructed for our survival, in that it was not meant for the survival of subaltern populations.

(Darder, 2015a)

And when we speak we are afraid our words will not be heard nor welcomed but when we are silent we are still afraid so it is better to speak remembering we were never meant to survive.

(Lorde, 2000)

For years I walked in silence. Seemingly, I was afraid to confront or name the conditions that had almost swallowed me whole, leaving little room for me to breath or speak out. After all, I figured, what right did I have to name societal problems; and moreover, who would listen to me? It was not until I was exposed to the writings of Paulo Freire, Antonia Darder, and other critical subaltern scholars, that I began to recognize that decolonizing praxis needed to evolve from the lived knowledge of the subaltern experience (Darder, 2015b, 2018). Consequently, I began to develop a language to more fully express the debilitating tensions and contradictions at work in the field of service learning, which I had constantly felt deeply within me but had remained silenced.

In my doctoral studies, I was first introduced to the writings of Paulo Freire. Enamored by Freire's beautiful pedagogy of truth and spirit, yet simultaneously angered by the reality that his work had only been introduced into my life in my late schooling, I embraced wholeheartedly the pedagogical and life dimensions of his writings. For someone who disliked reading all throughout my schooling, I experienced the writings of Freire and Darder as comforting transgressions and embodiments of political lives that were enveloped in a willingness to struggle and a refusal to live in vain.

Before reading *Pedagogy of the Oppressed* (Freire, 1970), I did not really have a conceptual understanding of what it meant to be oppressed or to live under structures that produce oppression. As I grappled to better understand Freire's ideas, I turned to Darder's *Culture and Power in the Classroom* (2012 [1991]) and *Reinventing Paulo Freire* (2002), books that engaged critical and cultural issues in the classroom as well as provided extensions and reinventions of Freire's writings. Darder's theoretical articulation of critical biculturalism and specifically what it meant to be bicultural—to be forced to constantly navigate the dialectical tensions between the dominant and subordinate culture—provided me with a deeper comprehension of Freire's view of the oppressed. Freire's oppressor–oppressed contradiction coupled with Darder's dominant–subordinate dialectic revealed for me a quest for a deeper understanding of my bicultural self, my communal relations with other bicultural workers, and the power of our collective voices and perspectives.

The veracity of Freire and Darder's philosophical claims provided me with a profoundly useful theoretical foundation, as I continuously re-read and studied their writings, over and over again, as a way to gain a deeper understanding, build new language, and simultaneously build the courage necessary to face what seemed to be daunting and impossible conditions of inequality. As Freire (1970) critically asserted, we need to be revolutionaries in our daily lives; not revolutionaries in the abstract. Contemplating what this meant for me, I realized that I had to be willing to change, to dream of new possibilities, and to bring a politically grounded critique to all facets of my work. Still, embracing Freire's work was layered in struggle, as I struggled to make sense of an educational practice I had participated in for almost a decade, while simultaneously reconciling it with a newly found evolutionary process of political clarity.

Awakening the subaltern voice

Through employing a decolonizing interpretive methodology, a process of political clarity began to unfold slowly in my work. As such, I began to engage more critically with my own experiences in the service learning field; yet, initially, this was difficult to enact as a living praxis. Through a process of reflection and dialogue with others, I became more acutely aware of the oppressive injustices that were at work within the service learning field and even began to articulate them well; but, somehow, I could not actualize this dimension fully in my work. Be it fear, lack of time, or being stuck within the confines of a structure/organization, a part of me was unwilling and tremendously terrified to do the work. I spent about a year in this space, before I came to a place where I was finally willing to let go of the fatalism and fear that was immobilizing me and fueling my inability to embrace change and the unknown. The critical examples of subaltern scholars and the recognition of my own social agency and power to participate in change led me to the cultivating and awakening of my subaltern voice—directly opposing the coloniality of power (Quijano, 2007) that impacts our lives at every level of our existence, including that of research.

Most mainstream researchers typically do not have an understanding of what it is like to be degraded and often inherently labeled as wretched (Fanon, 1963) based on historical racialized constructions of deficit. Our corporeality dictates how we are perceived in this world and, thus, how one must act in order to survive. For those of color, this corporeality is entrenched in inescapable historical processes of racialization at work at every level of our lives, which in turn denigrate the body and the soul. The colonization of the mind and body that results must be overcome but also recognized as a historical artifact—made by man and thus impermanent and changeable through our labor. Moreover, we must recognize that there have been and still are current and historically coordinated efforts that function to silence people of color from speaking up and against the "logics" of the dominant discourse.

Yet as within the context of a decolonizing interpretive approach, we must be able to courageously continue to confront the normalization of colonizing discourses. This entails entering into uncomfortable conversations related to race, gender, and all forms of oppression in order to more fully live our commitment to social justice. Resisting the commonsensical feature of dominant discourses is no easy task, as the view of what constitutes acceptable forms of research methodology is generally dictated by those in positions of power, blind to the colonizing epistemology that informs their values tied to research (Paraskeva, 2011). Consequently, as Linda Tuhiwai Smith (2012) rightly argues, in *Decolonizing Methodologies*, "many approaches to research remain insulated against the challenges of either indigenous research or stronger ethical protocols, and continue to see indigenous peoples, their values and practices as political hindrances that get in the way of good research" (p. 23).

Unveiling the colonizing roots of service learning

The awakening of the subaltern voice is not surprisingly linked with the growing capacity of subaltern researchers to unveil the colonizing roots of a phenomenon in which we both live and study. For example, from the standpoint of service learning's philanthropic roots, Césaire's (1972) writing reminds us that fundamentally Western civilization and its colonizing architects of charitable racism are ultimately inept at solving two major social problems: "the problem of the proletariat and the colonial problem" (p. 31). Few, if any, service learning researchers question the inexorable colonial relationship that exists within the service learning dynamic, even when radical, subaltern scholars have critically exposed the colonial logic that usurps and colonizes working-class populations (Césaire, 1972; Darder, 2012; Fanon, 1967; Freire, 1970; Memmi, 1965). Césaire (1972) called this structure into question, asserting that between colonization and civilization exists an infinite distance, wherein pseudo-humanism, racism, and sadistic pleasures that exoticize and exploit communities dwell.

Similarly, given the relentless insertion of service learning programs into working-class communities, this relationship—of colonizer and colonized (Memmi, 1965), oppressor and oppressed (Freire, 1970), or in the case of service learning, the cultural invader and the culturally invaded—steeped in disabling dependence, is rarely critically unveiled and challenged. About this, Albert Memmi (1965) notes, "the colonial rela-tionship … chained the colonizer and colonized into an implacable dependence, molded their respective characters and dictated their conduct" (p. ix). Accordingly, the colonizer repeatedly fails to see the misery of the colonized or even the relationship of this misery to the colonizer's own comfort (Memmi, 1965), which, as a consequence, serves to *decivilize* the colonizer (Césaire, 1972). Within the standpoint of decolonizing interpretive research, this failure to acknowledge the forces of hegemonic dependency that shape the lives of subaltern communities perpetuates false notions of distanced observers from our subject of study. This can be particularly debilitating and confusing to subaltern researchers who experience the dissonance of cultural conflict between institutional research expectations and community expectations that we serve as social justice advocates for our communities.

Further, within service learning, the colonizing relationship between those that are served and those that provide service (students, faculty, the institution, etc.) must also be critically engaged within the historical contexts of slavery, religious assimilation, and positivist-influenced disciplines that have imposed a series of negations upon those that are poor, "served," and oppressed. These colonizing negations, in short, advanced in the field as supposedly forms of denunciation of the injustices that plague communities, in fact, contribute to injustices by way of culturally invasive research practices, which deny the humanity of subaltern com-munities and chain them to a fate of eternal dependence. Hence, an important first step in the process of decolonizing interpretive research, as Darder posits, entails a process of unveiling hegemonic notions rooted in colonization—centering the subaltern voice serves as a means for this unveiling.

It is worth noting here that the concept of service has enjoyed historical longevity—rooted deeply within hegemonic institutions of the West (i.e., churches, schools/universities, government, military, etc.), reminiscent of indentured servitude, and rarely questioned as a colonizing practice that repro-duces oppression. Service learning lives in, moves in, and embeds itself within subaltern communities. It does not, in contrast, live in, move in, or embed itself in spaces of affluence. Hence, a praxis of decolonizing interpretive research requires that we name these conditions by no longer standing by and accepting the displacement of the oppressed, by way of a culturally invasive practice of service that purports to be for their well-being.

Despite the culturally invasive underpinnings of service learning, emergences of critical forms of service learning have still fallen short, as they forcefully uphold the structure of a one-sided, unidirectional practice, which fails to question why the privileged are never the recipients of "service" or in need of "help." From my study, this proved to be so because contemporary service learning literature had failed to provide a decolonizing examination of this educational archetype and pervasive "service" movement. While there have been efforts to articulate and actualize critical community service learning (e.g., D'Arlach et al., 2009; Daigre, 2000; Hart, 2006; Marullo & Edwards, 2000; Masucci & Renner, 2001; Mitchell, 2008; Seedat, 2012), many important aspects of analysis are missing from these reformulations in the field. Similarly, there is a dearth in the literature's engagement of service learning from the standpoint of subaltern concerns.

Alongside this recent emergence of critical literature in service learning, there has also been a subset of literature that proclaims the need for the voices of communities (Birdsall, 2005; Cruz & Giles, 2000; Stoecker & Tryon, 2009; Vernon & Ward, 1999) in service learning scholarship. Nevertheless, critical efforts "to hear" the voices of the oppressed or the "served" easily fall victim to manufactured abstractions and distortions of reality, which serve to sustain failed mainstream educational reform efforts of the past and uphold hierarchical and elitist educational structures of power. This then lends credence to Freire's assertion that the historical task of the oppressed is to work toward our own liberation (Darder, 2015b). Yet, unfortunately, the presence of decolonizing research voices has remained missing from the service learning literature, resulting in a lack of critical scholarship by people of color, whose voices are in solidarity with their own communities.

The politics of the subaltern voice

> The politics of the subaltern voice engages forthrightly with the phenomenon of human oppression and its debilitating historical impact upon the identities, social location, representations, and material conditions of oppressed populations.
>
> *(Darder, 2018)*

Voice often symbolizes the ideologies, values, and guiding philosophies that embed histories and cultures (Giroux, 1986). And thus, the use of voice is a political act, in that it can serve in the interests of the oppressed and/or act as a weaponized form of control. What Freire deeply understood about subaltern life is the manner in which the imposition of the colonizer's worldview and linguistic system upon the colonized was undoubtedly a formula for colonial domination. Consequently, making their own culture and language forms of estrangement to subaltern communities upholds the colonial project. Hence, "it is no coincidence that the colonizers speak of their own language as 'language' and the language of the colonized as 'dialect'" (Freire, 1978, pp. 50–51), conveniently inferiorizing its values and utility.

With the recognition that language is implicated in a structure of power relations, it is important to be aware of the political constructions that undergird discussions of voice in research circles. For in attempts to recognize and center subaltern voices in research and practice, subaltern voices are often co-opted, negated, and reconstructed in ways that conserve the epistemological comfort of those in power. This is no more evident than in the current mainstream "absence of voices" rhetoric (Darder, 2015b) that, as a consequence, runs the risk of tokenism and appropriation of the Other. In the service learning realm, the absences of voices rhetoric is employed widely in the empty and broken promises of the so-called honoring of subaltern communities as "co-educators" (Hernandez, 2018), given that those in positions of power claim to hear the voices of communities but rarely fully listen to or incorporate their offerings in the process of decision-making. Steeped in well-meaning intentions, this mainstream rhetoric is dangerous for subaltern researchers who sincerely wish to use their research to disrupt inequalities; yet, as a consequence, may find themselves being held to standards of watered down or euphemistic forms of knowledge production shaped by the politics of *model-token* or expert scholars of color (Hernandez, 2018).

According to Darder (2015b), a decolonizing interpretive methodology forth-rightly links the politics of voice to the "authority of our lived experience" (hooks, 1994), rooted in epistemological expressions of subaltern lives. In contrast, what generally exists within research is generated by the service learning movement, which serves as a staunch affirmation and privileging of Western epistemologies. As such, the voices of Eurocentric philosophers and scholars are given ample space within the canon to speak and with this legitimized space, they, deliberately or inadvertently, repress or silence critical bicultural voices, so that the subaltern are rendered voiceless and disposable. Furthermore, common discursive strategies leveled against subaltern voices—such as the distorting discourse of political cor-rectness—work further to silence, discourage, and marginalize decolonizing voices, even when speaking of phenomena deeply implicated in the lives of subaltern researchers themselves.

Thus, affirmation of the subaltern voice and the social agency associated with a politics of voice is essential here, given the hegemonic constraints of service learning that thwart the knowledge, wisdom, and power of subaltern communities. Deceptive notions of benevolent intentions and well-meaning mainstream discourses often serve to camouflage the colonizing inequalities that permeate the neoliberal arena of service learning—inequalities fueled by greed, exploitation, and practices of cultural invasion that strip the subaltern of our humanity. A decolonizing interpretive analysis then supports genuine conditions of empowerment that awaken the voices of subaltern communities, in a way that "cultivates their critical participation as active social agents in the world" (Darder, 2012, p. 44).

Toward a subaltern conceptual lens

A decolonizing interpretive approach requires that the researcher seek a conceptual lens that is in sync with subaltern sensibilities that drive their investigation. Darder (2014) suggests two important epistemological questions to consider when deciding to cite or engage the work of established theorists: "(1) [does it] genuinely speak to the heart of arguments born within our experience, and (2) [does it] illuminate the points we seek to make" (p. 195). This is noteworthy, given the epistemological omission of subaltern sensibilities within service learning research, which for example, signals a significant and dire gap that needs to be carefully unveiled and addressed in both practice and scholarly contexts.

In direct contrast, the subaltern conceptual lens that informs a critical bicultural pedagogy, as formulated by Darder in *Culture and Power in the Classroom* (2012 [1991]), was utilized to provide the necessary critical theoretical framework to tackle pedagogical implications, philosophical underpinnings, historical constructions, and asymmetrical power relations often at work within the ethos of service learning.

Referred to as a "superb exegesis" (Paraskeva, 2011), critical bicultural pedagogy "holds the possibility for a discourse of hope" and, thus, allows for subaltern researchers and practitioners within service learning to "question the structures of domination that control their lives" (Darder, 2012 [1991], p. 101).

Darder's (2012 [1991]) critical definition of biculturalism was essential to my interpretive decolonizing efforts to center the subaltern voice:

> Biculturalism speaks to the process wherein individuals learn to function in two distinct sociocultural environments: their primary culture, and that of the dominant mainstream culture of the society in which they live. It represents the process by which bicultural human beings mediate between the dominant discourse of educational institutions and the realities that they must face as members of subordinate cultures. More specifically, the process of biculturation incorporates the daily struggle with racism and other forms of cultural invasion.
>
> *(p. 45)*

As such, Darder's critical bicultural pedagogical lens, along with Smith's decolonizing methodology—both anchored uncompromisingly in a transformative praxis—infuses subaltern research with a necessary theory of resistance and critique that directly informs a decolonizing interpretive methodology.

Bicultural communities upon which service learning has been thrust have been historically oppressed populations, whose existence and conditions render them members of subordinate cultures (Darder, 2012 [1991]). Darder's critical conceptualization of the complex sphere of biculturalism is firmly grounded in the intersections of culture and power and the dominant–subordinate dialectic, by which power relations are exposed and bicultural affirmation is centered. Through creating this conceptual space for legitimate engagement of subaltern sensibilities, a decolonizing interpretive methodology functions to directly counter the hegemonic decentering of the bicultural voice (Darder, 2015b). This is crucial given that bicultural communities must navigate, conform, and adjust to the societal dominant mainstream values that permeate the Eurocentric practice of service learning and, as such, are often forced to negate the legitimacy of their cultural existence.

About this, Smith (2012), writing from the standpoint of her subalternity as a Maori researcher, asserts that the very term "research" is intimately tied to European imperialism and colonialism. She argues, "the word … 'research', is probably one of the dirtiest words in the indigenous world's vocabulary" (p. 22). For Smith (2012), methodology in the simplest form represents the theory of method, approach/technique used, or the reason employed to select a set of methods. This broad definition, however, Smith notes is of less concern; however, what is of importance with regard to methodology is the context in which the research problems are designed and conceptualized as well as its effects on communities. With regard to decolonizing methodologies, Smith suggests, "it is also concerned with the institution of research, its claims, its values and practices, and its relationships to power. It has 'talked back to' and 'talked up to' research as an institution of knowledge" (p. 20). Research then is fundamentally about what constitutes knowledge, who speaks and defines history, and what voices are heard and valued and which are relegated to the culture of silence (Freire, 1970). It is this hegemonic characteristic of knowledge construction that blatantly disregards non-Western epistemic traditions born out of the lived histories of subaltern survival.

Provoking subaltern epistemological shifts

Current critical conceptions and methodological analyses of service learning, like traditional notions of research, espouse a positivist ideology that is rooted in a Western paradigm. About this, Paraskeva (2011) critically notes, "Western counter-dominant perspectives are crucial in the struggle for social and cognitive justice, yet not enough" (p. xxi). He further insists that Western critical conceptions and theories must also open up the Western canon of protected knowledge and make way for new epistemological configurations. New epistemological configurations, however, would not be possible without a decolonizing methodology rooted in transformative possibilities (Darder, 2015b), in that the conservative educational policies and practices, as well as traditional discourses of research, are grounded in a positivist ideology, which views the world technocratically and is informed by a reductive scientific logic and method (Darder, 2012 [1991]).

Moreover, Darder (2015b, 2018) has posited in her seminal works on *decolonizing interpretive research*, that a decolonizing interpretive methodology is often poorly defined, seldom understood, and rarely discussed in established research methods courses offered by educational studies programs. These programs, steeped in an unacknowledged deficit lens, often discourage and rarely offer alternative research designs focused on theory building, particularly to students of color who are seldom "considered capable of such depth of analysis" (Darder, 2015b, p. 72). In contrast, Darder's (2015b) decolonizing interpretive research "is rooted in a critical approach that focuses on creating counterhegemonic intellectual spaces in which new readings of the world can unfold" (p. 1). Additionally, this decolonizing research approach unveils the asymmetrical structures of power and recognizes that all research practices are political processes and are never neutral, apolitical, or ahistorical. Accordingly, a decolonizing interpretive methodology seeks to assist subaltern researchers "to shift in both theory and practice the ways in which we comprehend ourselves and make sense of the world" (p. 3).

As a radical political project, a decolonizing interpretive framework—namely its theory building and autoethnographic dimensions—provide the grounding to systematically link practice to theory by way of a regenerative praxis (Darder, 2015b). This praxis, anchored in my lived experiences, for example, as a service learning educator and subaltern researcher, provided me an opportunity to center my voice in ways that could rupture the abyssal divide (Santos, 2007) that epistemologically privileges the Eurocentric service learning discourse, in an effort to place subaltern voices, scholarship, and communities at the center of this educational movement.

Moreover, it is in the rupturing of the abyssal divide and mobilization of an itinerant lens of analysis (Paraskeva, 2011) that an epistemological shift in consciousness is generated, anchored upon the interests of the oppressed, along with the affirmation of subaltern voices in the generation of decolonizing solutions to complex problems—solutions rooted in the histories, wisdom, and lived experiences of the subaltern. This also entails the asking of new questions and the critical engagement of oppressive conditions dialectically beyond focalization (Freire, 1970), in an effort to unveil oppressive epistemologies, articulate conceptual alternatives, and move toward the concrete transformation of hegemonic norms that drive hegemonic practices (Darder, 2015b).

Darder (2015) and Smith (2012) both also assert that a decolonizing methodology must seek a critical (re-)reading of the world, in a quest to unearth indigenous or subaltern histories and forms of knowing that have been formerly suppressed. Within the culture of service learning, dominant epistemologies have supported commonsense beliefs and practices that protect the interests of privileged actors. It is this hegemonic mechanism of knowledge construction, as noted earlier, that silences or dismisses non-Western epistemological traditions born out of lived histories of struggle. Furthermore, there is a powerful hegemonic apparatus that intersectionally perpetuate, reproduce, and reify classed, racialized, gendered, and heterosexist beliefs of the dominant society, limiting the legitimacy granted to contesting views of the Other (Fanon, 1967). As such, a decolonizing (re)formulation of service learning is systematically linked to critical research questions that seek to disrupt currently held values, beliefs, and assumptions, making room for new ways of understanding the phenomenon under study (Darder, 2015b).

A liberatory ethos

From a critical understanding, service too must be understood dialectically as a political act that can serve to liberate or oppress. It is the ideological myth of neutrality that frames and conceals service in sacrosanct and benevolent terms, that allows for oppressive forms of service to operate and rarely be perceived or posed as a problem (in the Freirean sense). To this point, questions of equity, ethics, and social justice unveil the phenomenon of service learning as a political act, including the use of language disruptions, such as the removal of the hyphen that typically exists in the term "service-learning." This liberatory ethos within the context of decolonizing research assists us to illuminate the work to be done in moving toward a reciprocal and co-constructed practice, beyond mere rhetorical proclamations and blind to social and material conditions that often negate the very existence of subaltern populations.

My interrogation of service learning, based on a decolonizing interpretive methodology, was nourished and developed the knowledge that evolved through centering a liberatory ethos. Hence, a major aim of my decolonizing interpretive work was to critically examine the field and develop a clear and systematic analysis to carefully unveil the contradictions within service learning, given the relentless insertion of service learning programs into poor working-class communities. Decolonizing service learning research requires enacting an emancipatory language of possibility, where possibilities may be conceived that have never entered the realm of consciousness or been spoken before, given our subaltern entrapment in hegemonic conceptions of service learning.

Thus, institutions employing service learning are called to thoroughly re-evaluate "business as usual," and seek to enact a liberatory ethos that honors and centers the voices of those served, in a genuine effort to work *with* rather than *for* communities. In contrast to what Freire (1970) called a "false generosity," my study concluded that the field of service learning must take up a genuinely empowering and humanizing generosity. Such a liberating ethos of practice does not seek to use "help" in ways that disempower and strip communities of their power, but rather recognizes that the solution for the oppressed must be collectively generated through their own transformative insights and efforts to liberate themselves—efforts generated from their histories of survival and everyday lives.

The laborious, methodological process of inquiry put forth in this decolonizing interpretive methodology also served as a powerful process of disruption and rupture of the oppressive discourses and practices of service learning. As such, my work illustrated that a much needed paradigmatic shift in both theory and practice would be required, in order to mobilize the field to critically engage the epistemicidal dimensions of dominant forms of service learning scholarship, policy, and practice. These knowledge-killing dimensions, as discussed above, have historically constructed and perpetuated commonsensical views, at the expense of indigenous and other subaltern communities—communities who can best speak of their conditions and generate solutions, first-hand, given they exist within the problems and conditions that must be transformed.

Beyond this, critical educators in positions of leadership and policy making within service learning must work to cultivate an organic and culturally democratic process of social change and the evolution of social consciousness as a dynamic communal process. This signals democratic policies and practices of voice and participation that nurture and cultivate the conscientization of men and women as free human beings. Sharpening and extending our decolonizing subaltern sensibilities within our research is also important to grounding our political commitment upon ethical liberatory principles that can unambiguously oppose all forms of oppressive practices that assault our dignity and obstruct our participation as subjects of history and cultural citizens of our world.

Critical to our understanding of the dialectic that exists between the individual voice and the collective voice is also a deeper understanding of ourselves and our roles as subaltern researchers, so that we can begin to epistemologically and paradigmatically shift the dialogue to one that critically interrogates the inability of traditional forms of research to disrupt and destroy the deeply rooted and concealed systems of domination that uphold and protect the colonizing interests of the ruling class. As Darder (2015b) contends, it is of paramount importance that subaltern researchers come to our decolonizing efforts with an acknowledgment that our individual voices exist dialectically *in relationship to* the collective voice of our communities. Accordingly, subaltern researchers must also "recognize that they are deeply accountable for the exercise of their individual voices" (p. 73). In our commitment to labor *with* the people, subaltern researchers must also embrace, as Freire (1970) espoused, our critical capacity to begin anew, to reinvent ourselves, to let go of the oppressive chains that bound our minds and bodies, as we consciously participate in an ongoing life process of becoming. Ultimately, this requires an enduring commitment to the people and to a larger political project of liberation.

Note

1 This chapter is based on my doctoral dissertation research entitled *Service Learning for Whom? Toward a Critical Decolonizing Bicultural Learning Pedagogy.* The study can be retrieved from https://pqdtopen.proquest.com/doc/1782296751.html?FMT=ABS.

References

Birdsall, J. T. (2005). Community voice: Community partners reflect on service learning. Retrieved from www.mc.maricopa.edu/other/engagement/Journal/Issue5/Birdsall.pdf.

Césaire, A. (1972). *Discourse on colonialism.* New York: Monthly Review Press.

Cruz, N., & Giles, D. (2000). Where's the community in service-learning research? *Michigan Journal of Community Service Learning* 7(Special Issue), 28–34.

Daigre, E. (2000). Toward a critical service-learning pedagogy: A Freirean approach to civic literacy. *Academic Exchange Quarterly* 4(4), 1–10. Retrieved from www.questia.com/library/journal/1G1-68362994/toward-a-critical-service-learning-pedagogy-a-freirean.

Darder, A. (2002). *Reinventing Paulo Freire: A pedagogy of love.* Boulder: Westview Press.

Darder, A. (2012 [1991]). *Culture and power in the classroom: A critical foundation for the education of bicultural students.* Boulder: Paradigm Press.

Darder, A. (2014). Epistemologies for a new world. In J. Paraskeva (Ed.), *Conflicts in curriculum theory: Challenging hegemonic epistemologies.* New York: Palgrave.

Darder, A. (2015a). From one never meant to survive. *Truthout,* May 6. Retrieved from https://truthout.org/articles/from-one-never-meant-to-survive/.

Darder, A. (2015b). Decolonizing interpretive research: A critical bicultural methodology for social change. *The International Education Journal: Comparative Perspectives* 14(2), 63–77. Retrieved from http://iejcomparative.org.

Darder, A. (2018). Decolonizing interpretive research: Subaltern sensibilities and the politics of voice. *Qualitative Research Journal* 18(2), 94–104.

D'Arlach, L., Sanchez, B., & Feuer, R. (2009). Voices from the community: A case for reciprocity in service-learning. *Michigan Journal of Community Service Learning* 16(1), 5–16. Retrieved from www.servicelearning.org/library/resource/8912.

Fanon, F. (1963). *The wretched of the earth.* New York: Grove Press.

Fanon, F. (1967). *Black skin, white masks.* London and Sydney: Pluto Press.

Freire, P. (1970). *Pedagogy of the oppressed.* New York: Seabury Press.

Freire, P. (1978). *Pedagogy in process: The letters to Guinea-Bissau.* New York: Seabury Press.

Giroux, H. (1986). Radical pedagogy and the politics of student voice. *Interchange* 17(1), 48–69.

Hart, S. (2006). Breaking literacy boundaries through critical service-learning: Education for the silenced and marginalized. *Mentoring and Tutoring: Partnership in Learning* 14, 17–32. http://dx.doi.org/10.1080/13611260500432236.

Hernandez, K. (2018). *Service learning as a political act in education: Bicultural foundations for a decolonizing pedagogy*. New York: Routledge.

hooks, b. (1994). *Teaching to transgress: Education as the practice of freedom*. New York: Routledge.

Lorde, A. (2000). *Collected poems of Audre Lorde*. New York: W. W. Norton & Co.

Marullo, S., & Edwards, B. (2000). From charity to justice: The potential of university community collaboration for social change. *American Behavioral Scientist* 43(5), 895–912.

Masucci, M., & Renner, A. (2001). Reading the lives of others: The Winton Homes Library Project—A cultural studies analysis of critical service learning for education. *The High School Journal* 84, 36–47.

Memmi, A. (1965). *The colonizer and the colonized*. Boston: Beacon.

Mitchell, T. (2008). Traditional vs. critical service-learning: Engaging the literature to differentiate two models. *Michigan Journal of Community Service* 14(2), 50–65. Retrieved from http://files.eric.ed.gov/fulltext/EJ831374.pdf.

Paraskeva, J. (2011). *Conflicts in curriculum theory: Challenging hegemonic epistemologies*. New York: Palgrave Macmillan.

Quijano, A. (2007). Coloniality and modernity/rationality. *Cultural Studies* 21(2–3), 168–178.

Santos, B. de Sousa (2007). Beyond abyssal thinking: From global lines to ecologies of knowledges. *Review* XXX(1), 45–89. Retrieved from www.boaventuradesousasantos. pt/media/pdfs/Beyond_Abyssal_Thinking_Review_2007.PDF.

Seedat, M. (2012). Community engagement as liberal performance, as critical intellectualism and as praxis. *Journal of Psychology in Africa* 22(4), 489–498.

Smith, L. T. (2012). *Decolonizing methodologies* (2nd edition). London: Zed Books.

Stoecker, R., & Tryon, E. (2009). *The unheard voices: Community organizations and service learning*. Philadelphia: Temple University Press.

Vernon, A., & Ward, K. (1999). Campus and community partnerships: Assessing impacts and strengthening connections. *Michigan Journal of Community Service Learning* 6, 30–37.

3

NAMING THE POLITICS OF COLONIALITY[1]

Emily Estioco Bautista

> Coloniality is paradoxically based in the tacit understanding that peoples, knowledges, and interconnectivity are always place-based. Coloniality created savagery in order to claim domain over it and the lands of which the then-named savages were living. Seeing this as paradoxical and self-serving logic helps to unsettle the terms on which settler colonialism is based and maintained. The paradox can be ascertained through its project of knowledge and for what purposes.
>
> *(Patel, 2016)*

Reading Paulo Freire's (1970) *Pedagogy of the Oppressed* in the context of an ethnic studies pedagogy (Tintiangco-Cubales et al., 2014) during my first year in college helped me re-read my Los Angeles public schooling experiences as an extension of the colonial project in the Philippines (my parents' country of origin) and as a subaltern subject in US schools serving minoritized communities. This re-reading was informed by Freire's (1970) analysis of "manipulation" as a characteristic of antidialogical action where manipulation is utilized as a means for dominant elites to "try to conform the masses to their objectives" (p. 147), which is often employed through "banking education"—a learning process that positions teachers as authorities on what is deemed knowledge and students as mere recipients of information that is banked into them.

Freire's impact on my thinking helped me understand how a Eurocentric curriculum throughout my K-12 schooling rendered the history of my ancestors invisible, while instilling in me the value of participating in Western epistemic ideologies in the pursuit of surviving within a capitalist economic context. As I began to understand how colonial education in the Philippines sustained imperialist interests to drain Philippine resources to benefit the US capitalist economy (Constantino, 2002), applying the principles of critical pedagogy (Darder et al., 2009) helped guide me on my journey to heal from the epistemic violence of colonial education (Mignolo, 2007) that spans across the globe.

Because ethnic studies courses facilitated my own process of critically understanding my positionality and my connection to the impacts of colonial imperialism, ethnic studies pedagogies informed my lifelong journey in the collective struggle for anti-racism, decolonization, and self-determination. As a student organizer, I helped lead campaigns to advance Pilipino Studies, sustain funding for student-initiated and student-run organizations, serving on-campus and local minoritized communities, and to elect philosophically aligned students into student government. Upon graduation from my undergraduate studies, I accepted a position as a secondary social studies teacher in order to continue my participation within the Los Angeles public schools in the political project of critical and ethnic studies pedagogies. As a secondary educator whose leadership development was cultivated in youth organizing spaces, I sought to create learning conditions where youth of color could become empowered in their identities and in their agency to impact the lived realities of their communities.

Simultaneously, I continued my activism in educator organizer spaces, where theoretical tensions regarding how to balance teacher-led and student-led spaces in Freedom School programming made the dialectical tension that Freire (1998) asserted between authority and freedom palpable. While my critique of the "ivory tower syndrome," where there is a clear distinction between academia and society whereby academics are disconnected from community (Chatterton et al., 2010), informed my resistance to pursue doctoral studies, the need for a space to cultivate a deeper intellectual engagement with the dialectical tensions that arose in my teaching and organizing spaces drove my decision to enter a doctoral program, with the intention of working with a philosophically aligned scholar in the field.

In my qualitative methods course, we examined hegemonic research notions in which only people who have mastered positivistic methodologies have the authority to generate knowledge around a neutral, uncontested "truth" (Denzin & Lincoln, 1994). Given that my scholarship is aligned with a critical perspective, where theory and practice are inextricably linked, research must be understood as a political act that resists dehumanizing tendencies; as such, marginalized groups are recognized and self-vigilance and reflection is key (Lindlof & Taylor, 2011). In the process of learning about qualitative studies, I was infuriated that the course insinuated that the only viable research I could engage in were ones that would ultimately require the distanced objectivity of a researcher, a methodology that would facilitate the very disconnection between academics and communities that I had worked to resist before entering graduate school.

However, this began to change for me when I began to engage with a decolonizing interpretive methodology, which introduced me to a methodology that was aligned with my critical pedagogical focus and, inherently honored my need for deep intellectual engagement into the logics of coloniality in my study of social movements and youth organizing pedagogies, along with my vision to develop a transformative youth organizing framework. Through Darder's approach to methodology and mentorship, I was able to engage in a decolonizing interpretive process grounded in my lived experiences as a subaltern scholar, while creating knowledge that could resist the colonial logics of Western epistemologies in the pursuit of an ethics of liberation (Darder, 2018). Moreover, as a scholar committed to a politics of decolonization and self-determination, naming the politics of coloniality in my research has been fundamental to my process of healing from the epistemological violence of hegemonic Western positivistic ideologies and practices.

The politics of coloniality

While the forceful and insidious processes of colonialism have taken place under varying contexts and conditions so that the decolonization process cannot be essentialized (Tuck & Yang, 2012), colonialism has been a consistent political means by which to implement and sustain the European imperial project around the globe (Smith, 1999). Here, I will discuss how naming the politics of coloniality is a critical component of decolonizing interpretive methodology, where an examination of literature with a critical lens unveils the impact of colonialism on epistemicides of indigenous ideologies (Quijano, 2007), knowledge production rooted in Western epistemologies (Mignolo, 2007), and the perpetuation of exploitative political economies (Chilcote, 2000), racism (Mignolo, 2007), heteropatriarchy (Arvin et al., 2013), and colonial education (Shahjahan et al., 2009) that sustain colonial power and privilege. True to principles of decolonizing methodology (Patel, 2016; Darder, 2015, 2018; Smith, 1999), there was little genuine possibility of transforming mainstream notions about youth movement organizing, without *naming the coloniality of power* in the process of my research.

Colonialism as vehicle for European imperialism

Indigenous scholar Linda Tuhiwai Smith (1999) countered Western approaches to knowledge production in her seminal work, *Decolonizing Methodologies*. Tracing the roots of the rising dominance of Western epistemologies in academia, Smith explored various explanations for imperialism: economic expansion, subjugation of others, imperialism as an idea, and imperialism as a field of knowledge. From an economic perspective, the later stages of 19th-century imperialism are tied to the challenges presented by the maturation of capitalism in Europe. As European consumers and workers could no longer afford and, thus, purchase the products being produced, European industrialists sought to shift their capital to new markets in order to secure their capital investments. When presented with this challenge during the advent of improved technologies to travel around the globe, various European countries funded expeditions to different lands in search of new resources and markets. Subtle nuances and stories of imperialism exist because various European nations had unique experiences with different indigenous peoples and, thus, different "sophisticated 'rules of practice'" (Smith, 1999, p. 22) were developed in order to subjugate the subaltern populations. These practices were critical to gaining access to new resources and markets to address the crisis in Europe's maturing capitalism.

Imperialism as an ideology is inextricably linked to the spirit of European conquest (Smith, 1999). Smith (1999) explored how because the Enlightenment period transformed economic, political, and cultural life toward new concepts of modernity, it facilitated new conceptions about the modern state, science, and even the "modern" human person. Imperialism not only provided a medium for economic expansion, it also provided opportunities to build new ideas and discoveries for science and political practice. The "imperial imagination enabled European nations to imagine the possibility that new worlds, new wealth and new possessions existed that could be discovered and controlled" (Smith, 1999, p. 22).

Thus, colonialism played a critical role in sustaining imperialist imaginations across the globe as colonies served as "a means to secure ports, access to raw materials and efficient transfer of commodities from point of origin to the imperial centre" (Smith, 1999, p. 23). While there was heterogeneity among European settlers in the colonies, the imperial imagination created a common desire to reimagine future nations that actualize Enlightenment ideals. Thus, colonies also served as cultural sites that attempted to represent Western ideas of civilization through a process of othering indigenous communities who did not match Western notions of civilization, which served to justify the subjugation and control of indigenous peoples, epistemologies, and lands.

Colonialism as a system of control

Colonialism as a system of control was, moreover, executed across a variety of social and material forces that consolidated the control of resources, economic wealth, and political power. As will be apparent in the following discussion, despite efforts to speak of these forces separately, it must be understood that they work as an interlocking system of coloniality and overlap is inherent in the exercise of control.

Control of land

Walter Mignolo (2007) argued securing capital was a critical component to solving Europe's economic crisis as capital is necessary for organizing labor, production, and distribution. Because "the appropriation of land *enormously increased the size and power of capital*" (Mignolo, 2007, p. 481, emphasis in original), land played a critical role in the development of a mercantile capitalist economy. The massive appropriation of land in the Americas created conditions where Europeans came to settle, indigenous civilizations were destroyed, indigenous peoples experienced genocide, and enslaved people from Africa were transported to replace the dying indigenous labor force. Colonial expansion provided for the creation of new societies through the plunder of land.

The "1877 theft of 7.7 million acres of treaty-protected lands in what was then called the Dakota Territories" (Cook-Lynn, 2007, p. 201), for example, is a critical moment between the United States and the First Nations, an event that demonstrates the colonial disregard and violation of indigenous sovereignty. The history of land theft had critical implications for the loss of resources which pushed subsequent tribal generations into poverty, colonial Christian-driven justifications for land dispossession such as Manifest Destiny rhetoric, and the failure to examine state-sanctioned genocide directed toward all North American tribal nations (Cook-Lynn, 2007). Additionally, because land was intrinsically connected to religion and spirituality, the dispossession of land worked to sever indigenous people's connections to their source of power, the spiritual strength that is the root of revolution (Alfred, 2015).

Control through force

In the Americas, colonial violence was also reflected in the genocide of natives, their exploitation as an expendable labor force, the spread of European diseases, and the violence of conquest (Quijano, 2007). Frantz Fanon (1963) describes colonial inter-actions between those positioned as colonizer and those as colonized as marked by "violence and their cohabitation—or rather the exploitation of the colonized by the colonizer—continued at the point of bayonet and under cannon fire" (p. 2). Not only was violence used to destroy civilizations in order to steal land, it was also used to exploit indigenous knowledge "in mining, agriculture, as well as their products and work" (Quijano, 2007, p. 169), all of which would ultimately serve European imperialist interests in the pursuit of economic expansion.

Additionally, Fanon (1963) argues that exploitation of the colonized was sustained through violence carried out by soldiers or police officers that served as legitimate representatives of the colonial regime. By keeping close scrutiny over the colonized and containing them through "rifle butts and napalm," these official agents of the state maintained the visibility of the colonizers' domination and played the role of law enforcers who brought "violence into the homes and minds of the colonized subject" (Fanon, 1963, p. 4). Freire (1970) described this process as the first characteristic of antidialogical action: the necessity for *conquest*, where an oppressor's goal is to conquer others through every means possible. Here, the oppressed "are dispossessed of their word, their expressiveness, their culture. Further, once a situation of oppression has been initiated, antidialogue becomes indispensable to its preservation" (p. 138). Conquest is reproduced and perpetuated through structures of subjugation in order to keep the conquered in a state of passivity and dependence.

Control of knowledge

As Fanon (1963) and Freire (1970) argue, colonial violence was not only physical but also took place in the minds and hearts of those who are oppressed. Colonialism repressed "specific beliefs, ideas, images, symbols or knowledge that were not useful to global colonial domination"; all of which, as Quijano (2007) argues, are "modes of knowing, producing knowledge, of producing perspectives, images and systems of images, symbols, modes of signification, over the resources, patterns, and instruments of formalized and objectivized expression, intellectual or visual" (p. 169). This form of repression was exacerbated by genocidal extermination of many indigenous populations. For example, in the region between "the Aztec-Maya-Caribbean and the Tawantinsuyana (or Inca) areas, about 65 million inhabitants were exterminated in a period of less than 50 years" (Quijano, 2007, p. 170), which also destroyed societies and cultures. The adverse consequences were marked by turning what were once high cultures in America into "illiterate, peasant subcultures condemned to orality" due to the survivors being "deprived of their own patterns of formalized, objectivized, intellectual, and plastic or visual expression" (Quijano, 2007, p. 170). This left many survivors with "no other modes of intellectual and plastic or visual formalized and objectivized expressions, but through the cultural patterns of the rulers, even if subverting them in certain cases to transmit other needs of expression" (Quijano, 2007, p. 170).

There is no question that this colonizing process led to the invasive imposition of the colonizer's patterns of expression, beliefs, and images. Boaventura de Sousa Santos (2014) refers to this process as *an epistemicide*, the systematic "murder of knowledge" (p. 92). Here, Santos asserts that there is an implied death of the subordinated culture's knowledge and the social groups that possessed that knowledge when unequal exchanges between different cultures exist. As indigenous epistemologies are destroyed, the process of epistemicide disqualifies social agents who operate according to indigenous modes of living aligned with indigenous epistemologies. By disqualifying, invisibilizing, and ultimately destroying different ways of knowing, those who commit epistemicide assert the dominance of their own epistemological canon, in order to assert power and privilege.

Scientific knowledge

As indigenous epistemologies become delegitimized through epistemicide, epistemological systems of the colonizer become inscribed as a hegemonic force. The Enlightenment period in Europe, as Santos (2014) notes, cultivated the development of empiricism, the theory that knowledge is derived from sense-experiences. As empiricist frameworks shaped European scholars' notions of how to produce knowledge, the scientific paradigm of positivism was created. People who ascribe to positivism posit that the world can be reduced to neutral measurements through the scientific method, which can reveal an objective knowledge and singular understanding of any scientific phenomena of interest (Hunter, 2002). According to the positivist tradition, as Smith (1999) maintains, not only can the natural world be examined and understood, but so too the social world of humans. These ideologies stemming from the Enlightenment period provide the foundation for academic systems grounded in Western contemporary understandings of who has the authority to wield scientific knowledge and through what methods the creation of legitimate knowledge is employed.

Instilling individualism

Colonialism sustains its power and structures through individualism. During the Enlightenment period, as Grosfoguel (2013) contends, Rene Descartes's famous phrase "I think, therefore I am" formed the basis for a Cartesian philosophy in which the "I," the individual, becomes a new source of knowledge, thus challenging Christian notions of God as the source of knowledge. From an ontologically dualist perspective, the mind has the ability to hold universal truths; from an epistemological standpoint, the individual has the capacity to hold internal monologues to arrive at objective knowledge that does not need to be situated within a historical or social context. In her work on *Red Pedagogy*, Sandy Grande (2004) moreover argues that Cartesian ontological and epistemological frameworks promote individualism by claiming that individuals can create knowledge independent of time and space, hence legitimating the decontextualization of knowledge.

Because capitalism creates conditions in which only a small minority of people can attain wealth through the labor of a vast majority, it is also bolstered by an ideology of individualism. Fanon (1963) supported this notion by claiming that one of the first Western values instilled in the colonized was individualism. He argued that the "colonized intellectual learned from his masters that the individual must assert himself" (p. 11). Furthermore, the "colonialist bourgeoisie hammered into the colonized mind the notion of a society of individuals where each is loved in his subjectivity, where wealth lies in thought" (p. 11). This illustrates the manner in which instilling individualism in colonized subjects was critical to sustaining perceptions of necessary survival tactics within the capitalist colonial context.

Individualism also impacts the ways in which people understand the rise of different social problems or concerns and possible modes of action. Freire (1970) argues that one of the characteristics of oppressive cultural action is an "emphasis on a *focalized* view of problems rather than on seeing them as dimensions of a *totality*" (p. 141, emphasis in original). By obscuring the role of larger systems and structures in oppressive realities by creating a focus on the role of individuals, a focalized view promotes alienation which, in turn, creates conditions where it is easier to keep people divided. Freire notes that these "focalized forms of action ... hamper the oppressed from perceiving reality critically and keep them isolated from the problems of oppressed women and men in other areas" (p. 141). By discouraging the masses from developing critical consciousness about the role of the ruling class through the lens of individualism, it functioned to prevent their unity. Thus, individualistic values preserve the status quo and make divide and conquer tactics an effective means for circumventing the unity of the oppressed.

Hegemony of religious knowledge

European Christianity also accompanied the imperial agenda for conquest. Since the notion of "I conquer, therefore I am" preceded Rene Descartes's assertion that "I think, therefore I am," Enrique Dussel (as cited in Grosfoguel, 2013) posits that the Cartesian philosophy is rooted in attitudes of conquest whereby people who have conquered the world place themselves at the center of the world, a process in which European conquerors believed they were able to acquire Christian "God-like" attributes. This shift, Mignolo (2007) argues, supported a secularization of Christianity, which converged with the rise of capitalism, imperialism, and the "hegemony of the Western world" (p. 460). Thus, during the rise of imperialism, the "Western politics of knowledge began to be imposed in Asia and Africa, in the nineteenth century" (p. 460). Additionally, *"control of knowledge in the Western Christendom belonged to Western Christian men, which meant the world would be conceived only from the perspective of Western Christian Men"* (Mignolo, 2007, p. 478, emphasis in original).

In the colonial context, European settlers characterized indigenous people as "evil" and feared becoming "poisoned and infected" once they "came into contact with the colonized" (Fanon, 1963, p. 7). Thus, Christianity became a weapon of resistance from what settlers deemed "evil" in the colonies. Furthermore, Fanon (1963) argued that the "Church in the colonies is a white man's Church" that "does not call the colonized to the ways of God, but to the ways of the white man, to the ways of the master, the ways of the oppressor" (p. 7). Here, religion was also a critical component of the colonial project to not only garner economic control but also obtain epistemological control over the native people of the colonies.

Viera Pawlíková-Vilhanová (2007) notes that Christians perceived that commerce with Africa was legitimate due to the belief that trade replaced the slave trade. The perceived shift to trade relationships legitimized Christian missionary activities that would expand moral and religious instruction as well as convert native "pagans" to the "true religion" (p. 253). Together, commerce and Christian activities helped facilitate what most abolitionists, humanitarians, philanthropists, and missionaries considered a prescription for the civilization and colonization of African societies. Anglican Protestant churches were driven to Christianize various parts of the world due to the belief that they were "deprived" of the message of the Gospel. Recognizing the existence of Catholic churches in Africa in the first centuries of the Christian era and in reaction to Protestant activity, Catholics were roused to bring about a reprise of missionary work in the 19th century. The expansion of the Christian missionary movement in Africa can be attributed to Christians' belief that they had a responsibility to regenerate the African peoples and an antislavery and humanitarianism conscience.

Catholic missionaries, according to Pawlíková-Vilhanová (2007), inscribed the Western cultural values they were products of into the practices, expectations, and culture of mission stations and schools. Instilled with the belief of the superiority of their Western culture, conversion was conflated with civilization efforts where Christian Western notions of morality imposed banning and abandoning some African customs such as polygamy, dancing, singing, and ancestor-worship. Distant boarding schools segregated and alienated converts from their families and societies while bringing them into closer proximity with Western culture as the emerging African elite that has embraced Western religion and cultural values.

Instilling heteropatriarchy

Colonial and Christian struggles over power and privilege also took place in terms of gender and sexuality. In the European Christian community, numerous and prominent nuns who were intellectuals interested in the principles of knowledge were chastised for participating in intellectual endeavors that were exclusive to men who were considered "the direct guardians of earth of God's knowledge" (Mignolo, 2007, p. 479). In this theological notion of gender roles, women were relegated to more subservient roles. In the colonial context, missionary settlers threatened by the power of female shamans in the Philippines, for example, would engage in subverting indigenous belief systems by transforming the narrative around indigenous symbols in ways that Menez (1996) asserts would: (1) demonize women and their sexuality promoting strict heteropatriarchal standards of "premarital chastity and marital fidelity" (p. 93); and (2) subjugate women under male authority by teaching "religion to young boys and adult males so that they could have better control of their women" (p. 93). In the Pilipino colonial context, these religious missionary efforts facilitated the shift of power, such that men were placed in privileged positions in households, akin to European values. These gender roles were also cultivated in the development of colonial administrations of indigenous populations, in which men were drawn into colonial government bodies.

Linguistic genocide

European imperial expansion also ushered forces that led to linguistic genocide of indigenous languages. The social and linguistic practices of colonial societies promoted the creation of a language hierarchy in which the colonizer's language is established as the superior, prestigious language used in governing administrative bodies and in economic activities; the demise of colonized peoples' languages through language displacement, language degeneration, language death, and linguicide; the creation of new languages; shifting the relationships between different local languages; and conditions where European and local languages had differing influences upon one another (Migge & Léglise, 2007). These language practices respectively created conditions in which: policies relegated local languages to fewer domains and elevated European languages to essential decision-making domains; attaining proficiency in the colonial language became critical to social mobility, which also pushed many colonized people to raise children in the colonial language; new languages were created, such as Creole and pidgin, in colonial contexts but were considered aberrations or corrupted versions of the colonial language; colonial decisions to conveniently designate one local language as the lingua franca promoted divide and conquer tactics; and the transformation of local languages by importing lexical material from the colonial language (Migge & Léglise, 2007).

When discussing the power of storytelling, Kenyan scholar Ngugi wa Thiong'o (1986) discusses how words and language have meaning beyond lexicon, since language provides symbols and images that reflect a unique worldview. Here, language is a medium of communication, culture, and collective memory. However, in missionary schools, and when the English colonial regime took control of schools in Kenya, English became the formal language of instruction in education. When recounting experiences in these schools, Thiong'o (1986) described how students caught speaking their native language would receive corporal punishment, other forms of public humiliation, or were even fined. Because economic and political control is not complete or effective without mental control, linguistic genocide subordinates people's culture and, thus, has served well as another vehicle for colonial control.

Instilling racism

During the secularization of Western Christianity, Mignolo (2007) argues that the "Western Christian men in control of knowledge were also White" and that thus, "in the sixteenth century a concept of *race* emerged at the intersection of faith, knowledge and skin color" (p. 479, emphasis in original). Mignolo (2007) and Grosfoguel (2013) discuss that in Spain, religious racism justified expelling the Muslim Moors and Jews. In the New World, the "Indians" had "created a crisis in Christian knowledge as to what kind of 'being' the 'Indians' would have" (Mignolo, 2007, p. 479) in the Christian hierarchy of beings. Supporting Fanon's analysis that indigenous peoples of colonized lands were deemed evil, Mignolo (2007) argues that because settlers believed they had the authority to determine where people belonged in the Christian hierarchy of beings, "Indians did not fit the standard model set by White Christian Men" and lacked "the legitimacy to classify people around the world" (p. 479); and, thus, declared indigenous people were inferior. White Christian men justified these claims by purporting that "Indians did not have 'religions' and whatever they believed was considered to be the work of the Devil" (p. 479). Because standards of humanity needed to fit within Christian religious and moral standards, whatever did not fit in terms of faith and physique was cast in a Christian hierarchy of being and, by the 15th century, became translated in terms of race.

The construct of race ultimately served imperial and colonial interests. The concept helped dehumanize enslaved and colonized groups and, thus, justified: access to indigenous lands (Grande, 2004); Christians' participation in the slave trade (Grosfoguel, 2013); and labor exploitation (Ross, 1982). Racism also served then as an epistemic operation that institutionalized the inferiority of indigenous peoples in the Americas and, subsequently, justified genocidal violence and the exploitation of their labor (Mignolo, 2007). Because genocide led to the death of millions of indigenous people, it created the need for a new labor force that promoted "the massive slave trade of Black African, many of them Moors, but darker skinned in comparison with the Indians and the North African Muslims that were expelled from Spain" (Mignolo, 2007, p. 479).

As the use of "'superficial' or phenotypical traits became the visible markers or significations of inferiority—the most apparent of which was skin color that contrasted with the pale skin of most Spaniards, mostly missionaries and red-haired soldiers as

Hernan Cortes" (Mignolo, 2007, p. 479)—race also became structured according to hierarchies. Notions of race became a source of scientific study in which race was attributable to inherited genes and fixed physical characteristics (Go, 2004; Memmi, 2000; Ross, 1982). Because race was understood as biologically unalterable, this ideology, along with the rise of Social Darwinism, supported Western ideations of their superiority in the purported racial hierarchy (Go, 2004) and subsequent referral of otherized races as barbarians (Cesaire, 1972).

Colonial education

Colonial schools in the colonies upheld Western ideations of civilizing the natives toward modernization (Mart, 2011; Pawlíková-Vilhanová, 2007), Western notions of racial inferiority (Cesaire, 1972; Fanon, 1963; Memmi, 2000; Said, 1979), and natives' assimilation into Western cultural values, practices, and sociopolitical structures (Grande, 2004; Mart, 2011; Nwanosike & Onyije, 2011). Colonial education assimilated colonized peoples by promoting the eradication of indigenous identities, languages, values, and customs through curricular epistemicides that privileged Western values (Grande, 2004; Mart, 2011; Nwanosike & Onyije, 2011; Paraskeva, 2016). In these colonial educational systems, colonial educators teach history in ways where the "history he writes is not the history of the country he is despoiling, but the history of his own nation's looting, raping, and starving to death" (Fanon, 1963, p. 15). As discussed above, students were oftentimes forbidden, punished, and shamed for speaking their native languages (Grande, 2004; Mart, 2011) and were sometimes even given new Western names (Willinsky, 1998). Christian missionaries and colonial administrations oftentimes created residential or boarding schools that aimed to alienate youth from their communities and cultural customs (Grande, 2004; Mart, 2011; Pawlíková-Vilhanová, 2007; Willinsky, 1998). Upon return to their communities, community members witnessed a loss of relationships and spirituality and a new sense of intolerance, competition, and arrogance (Mart, 2011).

Participation in Western colonial education promoted Western values of independence, achievement, competition, humanism that embraces objectivity, detachment from local and personal sources of knowledges, and detachment from nature (Grande, 2004). In the banking model of education, Freire (1970) notes that teachers fill students with information that is detached from wider experience, similar to oppressive cultural actions of divide and conquer tactics that attempt to mask the larger societal conditions that could spark unity, if people had a critical consciousness about their conditions. Thus, hegemonic schooling attempts to prevent the people, and their children, from developing a critical consciousness. Ultimately, this form of education serves oppressive, colonial interests to repress communities that might otherwise revolt and pursue liberation.

Colonial education systems, according to Willinsky (1998), signaled a shift from "imperial adventure to colonial consolidation" (p. 89), a symbol of colonial staying power. In the Philippines (Go, 2004) and India (Willinsky, 1998), colonial education maintained colonial relationships that benefited colonial powers by transforming natives into colonial intermediaries. Additionally, many colonial education systems taught colonial subjects the skills necessary for producing skilled labor for economic development (Mart, 2011). Colonial education was oftentimes marked by paternalism and restricted opportunities. Here, colonized subjects received limited education opportunities that would create a glass ceiling in their economic advancement and, thus, would not pose a threat to White advancement (Nwanosike & Onyije, 2011; Willinsky, 1998). As such, colonial education systems served to perpetuate the underdevelopment of colonized lands and a relationship of dependency between the colonial power and the colonized land.

Control of the political economy

Colonial powers sought to enjoy maximum economic benefits in the most cost-efficient way (Settles, 1996). When Europe began to participate in the African Slave Trade, the demand for labor not only stimulated the development of African systems of credit and exchange but also set the stage for subordinating the African economy according to European interests. Because some African states worked to build control over the international commerce that took place in their territories, they were able to demand high prices for goods. With the onset of the creation of European colonies in Africa, Europeans sought to exercise control over goods and drive the prices down (Settles, 1996). Thus, colonialism served to ensure direct political control in order to protect economic interests (Nwanosike & Onyije, 2011). By becoming a source for raw materials for Europe, initially for labor during the African Slave Trade and for cash crops during the period of "legitimate trade," and by becoming a consumer of goods due to colonial trade controls, Africa experienced the arrested development of technology and reduced freedom of choice in marketing goods (Settles, 1996).

Since colonies were expected to build the wealth of colonizing powers, Settles (1996) notes economic endeavors in the colonies were centered on sustaining their own internal development and administration. Revenue for colonial administrations was raised through taxing foreign trade and maintaining a central focus on building the export component of the economy. These colonial economic policies in Africa led to: the selective cultivation of crops for European interests and oftentimes the inadequacy of food reserves, chronic malnutrition, and famine in Africa; the rise of a large class of landless laborers; changes in patterns of work and gender roles, such that women and children were instrumental in the production system; and the disruption of traditional social structures. This created a legacy of Africa lacking parity as a "partner" in an international trade complex in which Africa is a net exporter of its own wealth.

As discussed above, the aim of capitalism is to control people's wealth, a process initiated through military conquest and followed by political dictatorship (Thiong'o, 1986). As evidenced by numerous countries around the globe that have experienced European colonization, another level of colonial control was exerted through political administration (Fanon, 1963). With the effective physical and cultural repression of indigenous populations through conquest, dispossession of land, military force, geno-cide, manipulation, and cultural invasion, Western settlers were able to maintain eco-nomic and ideological control through political decision-making in colonial administrative bodies. These political bodies enabled colonial governments to maintain control over labor and land's resources in ways that would ultimately serve imperial interests (Smith, 1999). Additionally, colonial administrative control over indigenous peoples was systematically maintained through acts of cultural invasion linked to colonizing educational systems (Freire, 1970; Pido, 1986; Thiong'o, 1986).

Coloniality in the contemporary moment

While the explicit political order of colonialism has been overturned in many countries, Quijano (2007) argues that coloniality "is still the most general form of domination in the world today" (p. 170). Thus, the legacy of ideologies instilled during colonial times remain intact and continue to impact the countries and people who have experienced colonial rule. Quijano (2007) further argues that coloniality operates through four interconnected domains, which Mignolo (2007) has referred to as the "colonial matrix of power." Tlostanova and Mignolo (2009) describe the *colonial matrix of power* as encompassing the following characteristics:

1   The struggle for the economic control (i.e. the appropriation of land, natural resources and exploitation of labor);
2   The struggle for the control of authority (setting up political organization, different forms of governmental, financial and legal systems, or the installation of military bases, as it happens today);
3   The control of the public sphere – among other ways, through the nuclear family (Christian or bourgeois), and the enforcing of normative sexuality and the naturalization of gender roles in relation to the system of authority and principles regulating economic practices. It is based on sexual normativity and dual "natural" gender relations;
4   The control of knowledge and subjectivity through education and colo-nizing the existing knowledges, which is the key and fundamental sphere of control that makes domination possible.

(p. 135)

The colonial matrix of power connects then to the current impact of coloniality such as: class privilege, individualism, racism, heteropatriarchy, and the politics of knowledge production and dissemination within education.

Social class

In the era of monopoly capitalism and imperialism, contemporary development faces varied obstacles (Chilcote, 2000). Andre Frank built on Baran's work by positing that the expropriation of economic surplus in capitalism promotes the development of metropolitan centers, former colonial powers, and the underdevelopment in peripheral satellites, former colonies (as cited in Chilcote, 2000). Pablo Casanova (as cited in Chilcote, 2000) argues that internal colonialism also takes place when ruling, dominant groups within a society dominate capital in ways that lead to the underdevelopment of marginal satellites and the subsequent exploitation of marginal groups.

Ronald Chilcote (2000) notes that discussions centered on world systems, internationalization of capital, post-imperialism, and globalization theories focus on international implications of capitalism. He argues that globalization theories serve to direct attention away from imperialism and create the impression that the capitalist world is rapidly advancing in a unified and harmonious way and that concerns related to social class are unnecessary preoccupations. About this, Samir Amin (2000) asserts globalization is "an ideological discourse used to legitimize the strategies of imperialist capital" (p. 157) and promotes the expansion of a polarizing capitalism that perpetuates inequality. Amin further posits that conditions of neoliberalism—the current phase of advanced capitalism—benefits the wealthy, divests the state from public interests, obfuscates social class, and undermines the work of regional organizations and unity. However, Amin also suggests that the political economic tensions resulting from globalization have also provoked popular protest and stimulated current struggles against increasing monopolies and contemporary forms of imperialism around the world.

Because imperial and colonial pursuits have the potential of increasing wealth in the context of capitalist economies, settler interests have been driven by wealth and class status, which have also dominated and continue to dominate politics and structures of former and current colonies. Fanon (1963) argues that class division, labor exploitation, and social hierarchies of status represented different practices of power. Thus, as settlers sought opportunities for power and economic self-advancement, these different practices of power were essential to helping them attain and maintain power and class privilege in the colonies, practices that oftentimes remained even after former colonial administrations were overturned. Darder (2003) notes that Freire was grounded in Marxist-Socialist thought, whereby his references to the ruling class or oppressors referred "to historical class distinctions and class conflict within the structure of capitalist society," an analysis that ultimately posits that "capitalism was the root of domination" (p. 501). Darder further argues that Freire's "theoretical analysis was fundamentally rooted in notions of class formation, particularly with respect to how the national political economy relegated the greater majority of its workers to an exploited and marginalized class" (p. 501).

Thus, the historical process of class formation created the current political economic conditions, in which a vast majority of workers are exploited and marginalized in order to serve the interest of the dominant, ruling class. This complex is evident today in how the maturation of capitalism into neoliberalism has produced an even wider divide between the ruling class and the oppressed. That is why Darder (2003) asserts that Freire "insisted that the struggle against oppression was a human struggle in which we had to build solidarity across our differences, if we were to change a world engulfed by capitalism" (p. 501).

Racism

Albert Memmi (2000) argues that the content of racism does not matter as much as the structure and the social relations that it creates. He further posits that the underlying ideologies of "raciology," or eugenics, exist to rationalize "heterophobia," the fear of any form of real or imaginary difference between groups. Thus, racism, as a contemporary structure, supports negative notions or implications of difference, applying repressive personal prejudice toward those who are considered different, resulting in the interpersonal mistreatment of those othered, while enlisting and enforcing negative perceptions to justify institutional hostility and aggression. The structure of racism, therefore, inversely promotes the construction of a positive or superior identity to those not considered different (Memmi, 2000).

The structure of racism is also institutionalized in government policies and legal structures that impact people on an individual level (Go, 2004; Memmi, 2000). The Southern White backlash to American Reconstruction-era advancements for African Americans produced Jim Crow laws that served to disenfranchise, criminalize, and re-enslave African Americans (Alexander, 2010). The structures of racism also have an impact on education policies and the curriculum children received in schools (Paraskeva, 2016). For example, in the literature children read, White children learn to associate Black with evil, fear, and depravity, while Black children learn to identify White figures as heroes who are pure, virtuous, and intelligent (Derman-Sparks & Edwards, 2009; Butts, 1979). Robert Ross (1982) argues that the ideology and structure of racism created conditions whereby colonized groups have come to internalize racism. However, Cesaire (1972) argues that Black people who resist the fallacy of racial inferiority can adopt "negritude," a concrete consciousness of Black identity pride grounded in Black history and a culture of great value and beauty, an identity worthy of dignity and respect.

In his analysis, Mignolo (2007) posits that in the colonies and prior to the Industrial Revolution, race was what class became after the Industrial Revolution in Europe. In Fanon's (1963) discussion of the superstructure in the colonies, he also argues that race and class are inextricably linked. He argues that divisions are determined by the race to which people are considered belonging. When looking at the economic infrastructure in the colonies, Fanon further notes that it is also a superstructure such that "you are rich because you are white, you are white because you are rich" (Fanon, 1963, p. 5). Thus, Freire's ideas become important to consider in current-day resistance efforts. Darder (2003) argues that many critical educators of color in the United States often view "racism as the major culprit of our oppression" (p. 501) without engaging the totalizing impact of capitalism on our lives. However, when Freire was engaged in discussions on race, he also cautioned critical educators of color against losing sight of the ways class is hidden in sexual and racial discrimination (Darder, 2003). Thus, while independent explorations of class and race can help explain coloniality in current contexts, it is also important to view the ways in which these forces intersect.

Heteropatriarchy

Patriarchy is based on a gender binary system in which one gender dominates the other (Smith, 2016). Heteropatriarchy refers to social systems in which "hetero-sexuality and patriarchy are perceived as normal and natural, and in which other configurations are perceived as abnormal, aberrant, and abhorrent" (Arvin et al., 2013). The biological dimorphism assumed by heteropatriarchy impacts people who do not identify within systematized gender and sexual binaries. When Western epistemologies privilege scientific and biological notions of gender and sexuality and apply their logic to government bodies, laws fail to serve intersexed individuals (Lugones, 2008).

The secularization of Christian values is evident in government policies wherein heteropatriarchy operates as "the building block of the nation-state form of govern-ance" (Smith, 2016, p. 270). Christian Right activist Charles Colson (as cited in Smith, 2016) used heterosexist rhetoric when he referred to marriage as "the traditional building block of human society," wherein "There is a natural moral order for the family … led by a married mother and father" (p. 270). Also, by stating that "Marriage is not a private institution … If we fail to enact a Federal Marriage Amendment, we can expect not just more family breakdown, but also more criminals behind bars" (p. 270), Colson claims that the health of the United States is intertwined with het-eropatriarchal notions of family. Ann Burlein (as cited in Smith, 2016) argues that Christian Right politics in the United States work to create a "Christian America" by centering the private family. By centering the private family, the Christian Right shifts focus away from public disinvestments. The Christian Right interprets the resulting social decay as deviance from heteropatriarchal ideologies instead of political and eco-nomic forces. Thus, heteropatriarchy serves as a building block and preserving force for imperialism, by imposing heteropatriarchal relations between the nation-state/empire and citizens/colonized peoples akin to patriarchs and families (Smith, 2016).

Colonizing education

In the current era of neoliberal economics, João Paraskeva (2016) argues that the education system and its curricula are implicated in the Eurocentrism and the colonial matrix of power and thus perpetuate epistemicides (Grosfoguel, 2013). He further argues that curricula that serve to legitimate and privilege Eurocentric ideas, values, and histories as official forms of knowledge are a form of curriculum epistemicide, a process that secures ideological control and is a capital crime against humanity. In the academy, the objectivist paradigm and over-emphasis on rationality (Shahjahan et al., 2009) perpetuates the repression of indigenous epistemologies and spiritual beliefs. This persistent epistemic privilege of the West is well-reflected in Ramon Grosfoguel's (2013) observation that "the canon of thought in all the disciplines of the Social Sci-ences and Humanities in the *Westernized University* is based on knowledge produced by a few men in five countries in Western Europe (Italy, France, England, Germany and the USA)" (p. 74, emphasis in original).

As early as the 1930s, African American scholar Carter G. Woodson (1933) argued that the education system served the interests of the privileged class and perpetuated the oppressed acceptance of social inequities linked to their "miseducation." Similarly, abroad, American educational policies in former colonies, such as the Philippines, aimed to assimilate the colonized populace to serve American economic interests (Constantino, 2002). In the current educational context, divestment from communities of color, poverty, lack of social supports, limited early learning opportunities, unequal access to qualified teachers, lack of access to high-quality curriculum, and dysfunctional learning environments contribute to the continued inequality that communities of color experience in the United States (Darling-Hammond, 2010).

Together, these inequitable *neocolonial*—a term that refers to the continued impact of former colonial experiences (Altbach, 1994)—educational experiences dehumanize youth of color by denying them the opportunity to engage in praxis—the ability to simultaneously act and reflect on their world (Freire, 1970); creating impersonal learning environments (Darling-Hammond, 2010); promoting conditions that limit access to resources to address symptoms of Complex Posttraumatic Stress Disorder[2] associated with living in poverty (Duncan-Andrade, 2014), and reinforcing White supremacist values that shame students of color (hooks, 2003).

Naming the politics of coloniality: implications for research

As illustrated above, naming the politics of coloniality is critical to a decolonizing approach to interpretive research. My discussion has sought to demonstrate how colonialism deeply impacts various intersections across race, class, gender, and sexuality through political economic systems, cultural and social practices, and epistemological and ontological approaches to knowledge production, giving further credence to the insistence that we engage with the coloniality of power, if we are to disrupt structures of thought that preserve all forms of injustice (Patel, 2016; Darder, 2015, 2018; Smith, 1999). Within the context of our decolonizing interpretive studies, naming the politics of coloniality helps unveil the deeply embedded colonial logic in positivist research traditions that deem theory as abstract and independent of lived realities or that bifurcate theory from practice. Naming the politics of coloniality in decolonizing interpretive research brings to light the epistemological violence inflicted on indigenous communities and their descendants who continue to be affected by the persistence of contemporary coloniality. By asserting that theory created by subaltern scholars is inextricably tied to their lives, decolonizing interpretive methodology situates our right to honor our lived experiences and the knowledge that it affords to our rethinking of social phenomenon within subaltern communities (Darder, 2018).

My research journey into the question of social movements and youth organizing, in particular, was inextricably grounded in a lived experience that led me to engage deeply with how decolonizing pedagogies in social movements could inform educators working to build intergenerational spaces for a liberatory education. Because my teaching and organizing spaces were not meeting my needs for a disciplined, deep inquiry of social movements and youth organizing; and because I felt traditional qualitative research methods would only jeopardize the sanctity of my relationships to my teaching and my organizing community praxis, decolonizing interpretive research methodology was best suited to meet my capacity and need, as a subaltern researcher, to explore extensive bodies of literature with a critical lens, in order to achieve a deeply nuanced understanding of the intersections of the logics of coloniality, social movement theories, and youth organizing pedagogies.

By exploring the logics of coloniality, social movement theories, and youth organizing pedagogies through a decolonizing interpretive methodology, I was able to glean that social movement theories and attending youth organizing pedagogies are so deeply embedded within Western ideologies that the epistemicidal "abyssal divide" (Santos, 2014) exists in these fields, so much so that the role of spirituality and indigenous values, for example, are rendered invisible. Because spiritual practices often sustain various indigenous epistemologies that counter Western sensibilities, many contemporary social movement and community organizing methodologies serve to further alienate colonized peoples from ancestral spiritual practices of power that could support their efforts to (1) abolish and move away from the colonial conditions that produce their oppression and (2) create the transformative and liberatory relationships and societies they seek. This key understanding that arose from a decolonizing interpretive research method provided me, as a subaltern researcher, a fundamental thread into the principles of the transformative youth organizing vision that emerged from my doctoral studies.

More importantly, in naming the politics of coloniality, the counterhegemonic project of a decolonizing interpretive methodology would be brushed against the epistemological violence of Western ideologies, which are often perpetuated by both quantitative and qualitative research approaches within the academy (Darder, 2015). Bringing a serious and nuanced understanding of the politics of coloniality to my work helped me to substantiate a process by which to critically question mainstream commitments to positivist knowledge production. A decolonizing interpretive methodology genuinely seeks to transform how subaltern scholars build knowledge and extend to us the right to do so, whether as teachers, doctoral students, or established scholars in the field. By disrupting the ubiquitous normalization of colonial, Western, Eurocentric sensibilities, subaltern decolonizing interpretive scholars find a place to create for the plurality of discourse (Paraskeva, 2016; Patel, 2016; Darder, 2015, 2018) necessary to our well-being, which inform in new ways how decolonizing scholarship can assist us to transform practice and consciousness out in the world.

Notes

1 This chapter is based on my doctoral dissertation research entitled *Transformative Youth Organizing: A Decolonizing Social Movement Framework*. The study can be retrieved from https://pqdtopen.proquest.com/doc/2033866592.html?FMT=ABS.

2 Jeff Duncan-Andrade builds on medical research on Complex Posttraumatic Stress Disorder (PTSD), a more complex form of long-term PTSD, and argues that young people residing in inner cities experience Complex PTSD due to recurring exposure to trauma, unlike war veterans who have left the region(s) where trauma was experienced.

References

Alexander, M. (2010). *The new Jim Crow: Mass incarceration in the age of colorblindness*. New York: The New Press.

Alfred, T. (2015). *Wasase: Indigenous pathways of action and freedom*. Tonawanda: University of Toronto Press.

Altbach, P. (1994). Education and neocolonialism. In B. Ashcroft, G. Griffiths, & H. Tiffin (Eds.), *The post-colonial studies reader* (pp. 452–456). New York: Routledge.

Amin, S. (2000). Capitalism, imperialism, globalization. In R. H. Chilcote (Ed.), *The political economy of imperialism: Critical appraisals* (pp. 157–168). Lanham: Rowman & Littlefield.

Arvin, M., Tuck, E., & Morrill, A. (2013). Decolonising feminism: Challenging connections between settler colonialism and heteropatriarchy. *Feminist Formations* 25(1), 8–34.

Butts, H. F. (1979). Frantz Fanon's contribution to psychiatry: The psychology of racism and colonialism. *Journal of the National Medical Association* 71(10), 1015–1018.

Cesaire, A. (1972). *Discourse on colonialism*. New York: MR.

Chatterton, P., Hodkinson, S., & Pickerill, J. (2010). Beyond scholar activism: Making strategic interventions inside and outside the neoliberal university. *ACME: An International E-Journal for Critical Geographies* 9(2), 245–275.

Chilcote, R. H. (2000). *The political economy of imperialism: Critical appraisals*. Lanham: Rowman & Littlefield.

Constantino, R. (2002). The miseducation of the Filipino. In A. V. Shaw & L. H. Francis (Eds.), *Vestiges of war: The Philippine-American war and the aftermath of an imperial dream, 1899–1999* (pp. 177–192). New York: New York University Press.

Cook-Lynn, E. (2004). Twentieth-century American Indian political dissent and Russell Means. *Wicazo Sa Review*, 14–18.

Cook-Lynn, E. (2007). *New Indians, old wars*. Chicago: University of Illinois Press.

Darder, A. (2003). Teaching as an act of love: Reflections on Paulo Freire and his contributions to our lives. In A. Darder, R. Torres, & M. Baltodano (Eds.), *The critical pedagogy reader* (pp. 497–511). New York: Routledge Falmer.

Darder, A. (2015). Decolonizing interpretive research: A critical bicultural methodology for social change. *The International Education Journal: Comparative Perspectives* 14(2), 63–77.

Darder, A. (2018). Decolonizing interpretive research: Subaltern sensibilities and the politics of voice. *Qualitative Research Journal* 18(2), 94–104.

Darder, A., Baltodano, M. P., & Torres, R. D. (2009). *The critical pedagogy reader*. New York: Routledge.

Darling-Hammond, L. (2010). *The flat world and education: How America's commitment to equity will determine our future*. New York: Teacher's College.

Denzin, N., & Lincoln, Y. (1994). Introduction: Entering the field of qualitative research. In N. Denzin & Y. Lincoln (Eds.), *Handbook of qualitative research* (pp. 1–17). Thousand Oaks: Sage.

Derman-Sparks, L., & Edwards, J. O. (2009). *Anti-bias education for young children and ourselves*. Washington, DC: National Association of the Education of Young Children.

Duncan-Andrade, J. (2014). Note to educators: Hope required when growing roses in concrete [Powerpoint slides]. Retrieved from www.google.com/url?sa=t&source=web&rct=j&url=https://mcli.maricopa.edu/files/success/2011/Keynote%2520Presentation%2520Duncan%2520Andrade.pdf&ved=0CC8QFjAFahUKEwjCyJPZkILHAhWH2D4KHQpKB-g&usg=AFQjCNGMMS3Yzvxz1z6VV3hjRUoFc4Wwaw&sig2=r7CE42n4lU1hCwtvSjDksw.

Fanon, F. (1963). *The wretched of the earth*. New York: Grove Press.

Freire, P. (1970). *Pedagogy of the oppressed*. New York: Herder and Herder.

Freire, P. (1998). *Pedagogy of freedom: Ethics, democracy, and civic courage*. New York: Rowman & Littlefield.

Go, J. (2004). "Racism" and colonialism: Meanings of difference and ruling practices in America's Pacific empire. *Qualitative Sociology* 27(1), 35–58.

Grande, S. (2004). *Red pedagogy: Native American social and political thought.* Lanham: Rowman & Littlefield.

Grosfoguel, R. (2013). The structure of knowledge in the westernized universities: Epistemic racism/sexism and the four genocides/epistemicides of the long 16th century. *Human Architecture: Journal of the Sociology of Self-Knowledge* 11(1), 73–90.

hooks, b. (2003). *Teaching community: A pedagogy of hope.* New York: Routledge.

Hunter, M. (2002). Rethinking epistemology, methodology, and racism: Or, is white sociology really dead? *Race & Society* 5, 119–138.

Lindlof, T., & Taylor, B. (2011). Theoretical traditions and qualitative communication research. In *Qualitative communication research methods* (pp. 33–70). Los Angeles: Sage.

Lugones, M. (2008). The coloniality of gender. *Worlds & Knowledges Otherwise*, 1–17.

Mart, Ç. T. (2011). British colonial education policy in Africa. *International Journal of English and Literature* 2(9), 190–194.

Memmi, A. (2000). *Racism.* Minneapolis: University of Minnesota Press.

Menez, H. Q. (1996). *Explorations in Philippine folklore.* Quezon City: Anteneo de Manila University Press.

Migge, B., & Léglise, I. (2007). Language and colonialism: Applied linguistics in the context of creole communities. In M. Hellinger and A. Pauwels (Eds.), *Language and communication: Diversity and change. Handbook of applied linguistics* (pp. 297–338). Berlin: Mouton de Gruyter.

Mignolo, W. D. (2007). Delinking: The rhetoric of modernity, the logic of coloniality and the grammar of de-coloniality. *Cultural Studies* 21(2), 449–514.

Nwanosike, O. F., & Onyije, L. E. (2011). Colonialism and education. International Conference on Teaching, Learning and Change, 2011, 624–631.

Paraskeva, J. M. (2016). *Curriculum epistemicide: Towards an itinerant curriculum theory.* New York: Routledge.

Patel, L. (2016). *Decolonizing educational research: From ownership to answerability.* New York: Routledge.

Pawlikova-Vilhanová, V. (2007). Christian missions in Africa and their role in the transformation of African societies. *Asian and African Studies*, 16(2), 249–260.

Pido, A. (1986). *The Pilipinos in America.* New York: Center for Migration Studies.

Quijano, A. (2007). Coloniality and modernity/rationality. *Cultural Studies* 21(2–3), 168–178.

Ross, R. (1982). *Racism and colonialism: Essays on ideology and social structure.* Hingham, MA: Martinus Nijhoff.

Said, E. W. (1979). *Orientalism.* New York: Vintage Books.

Santos, B. de Sousa (2014). *Epistemologies of the south: Justice against epistemicide.* Boulder: Paradigm Publishers.

Settles, J. D. (1996). *The impact of colonialism on African economic development* (Unpublished honors thesis project). University of Tennessee, Knoxville, TN.

Shahjahan, R. A., Wagner, A., & Wane, N. N. (2009). Rekindling the sacred: Toward a decolonizing pedagogy in higher education. *Journal of Thought*, 59–75.

Smith, A. (2016). Heteropatriarchy and the three pillars of White supremacy. In INCITE! Women of Color Against Violence (Ed.), *Color of violence: The INCITE! anthology* (pp. 66–73). Cambridge, MA: Duke University Press.

Smith, L. T. (1999). *Decolonizing methodologies: Research and indigenous peoples.* New York: Zed Books.

Thiong'o, N. (1986). *Decolonising the mind: The politics of language in African literature.* London: J. Currey.

Tintiangco-Cubales, A., Kohli, R., Sacramento, J., Henning, N., Agarwal-Rangnath, R., & Sleeter, C. (2014). Toward an ethnic studies pedagogy: Implications for K-12 schools from the research. *The Urban Review* 47(1), 104–125.

Tlostanova, M. V., & Mignolo, W. D. (2009). Global coloniality and the decolonial option. *Kult* 6, 130–147.

Tuck, E., & Yang, K. W. (2012). Decolonization is not a metaphor. *Decolonization: Indigeneity, Education & Society* 1(1), 1–40.

Willinsky, J. (1998). *Learning to divide the world: Education at the empire's end*. Minneapolis: University of Minnesota Press.

Woodson, C. G. (1933). *The miseducation of the Negro*. Washington, DC: Associated Publisher.

4

DEMYTHOLOGIZING HEGEMONIC BELIEFS[1]

Kenzo Bergeron

You can't be afraid of words that speak the truth, even if it's an unpleasant truth like the fact that there's a bigot and a racist in every living room and on every street corner in this country. I don't like words that hide the truth, I don't like words that conceal reality, I don't like euphemisms, or euphemistic language, and, American English is loaded with euphemisms because Americans have a lot of trouble dealing with reality. Americans have trouble facing the truth. So, they invented a kind soft language to protect themselves from it.

(Carlin, 1990)

In the dwindling minutes of game two of the 1991 NBA finals, Michael Jordan cuts through the lane and springs toward the basket. The nearest Lakers defender, Sam Perkins, does his best to contest the shot but Jordan simply recalibrates in midair and instead of delivering the anticipated dunk, gently banks the ball off the glass and into the basket. It happens in a flash. While players on the court and spectators in the arena seem to realize, instantly, the gravity of what they have just seen, at home I needed the assistance of a slow-motion replay. At school the next day, "The Move"—as it would famously come to be known—would be reenacted for whomever would listen and watch. Playing the part of Jordan, I jumped off of the long low benches that were scattered across the sprawling asphalt playground, waving my hands in the air in a sorry attempt to mimic what I had seen the night before.

Surely, I wasn't the only kid who idolized Jordan. In fact, 1991 was a banner year for the future hall of famer, and he would discuss the ingredients to his success— unmatched work ethic, infinite amounts of intensity, and a competitive compulsion— in an appearance on Oprah. After winning the NBA title, and his first finals MVP, Jordan's commercial popularity would also exponentially surge, in large part due to the Nike "It's Gotta Be the Shoes!" ad campaign. And by that Fall, Jordan was slated to do what we have all come to expect of any major sports MVP—host the season premiere of *Saturday Night Live*, a sketch comedy show entering its seventeenth season. In the early 1990s, *Saturday Night Live* featured a steady rotation of "Wayne's World," "Coffee Talk," and the androgynous character "Pat," and for the most part, Jordan's September 28 appearance does not stand out in any particular way. But, buried in the usual rotation of sketches was one titled, "Daily Affirmation with Stuart Smalley."

"Daily Affirmation" begins with stock footage of rolling clouds as, one by one, headshots float across the screen. Pictured is a blonde man with a lackluster sub-urban coif, modeling a potpourri of button downs and cardigans. Over the photo montage, a voice the viewer will soon recognize as Smalley's, in a cadence matching that of any generic guided meditation says, "I deserve good things. I am entitled to my share of happiness. I refuse to beat myself up. I am an attractive person. I am fun to be with." Finally, the title card dissolves, and the audience—via the voice of Phil Hartman—is introduced to "Daily Affirmation with Stuart Smalley." The title fades out and the camera pans over to Stuart Smalley, who is sitting on a couch looking at his reflection in an awkwardly placed cheval floor mirror. While a flute plays gently in the background, Hartman's voiceover con-tinues: "Stuart Smalley is a caring nurturer. A member of several twelve-step programs, but not a licensed therapist" (Downey, 1991). And as the voiceover fades out, Smalley chimes in, "I'm going to do a terrific show today and I'm going to help people because I'm good enough, I'm smart enough, and doggone it, people like me" (Downey, 1991).

Smalley introduces his guest, Michael J.—he insists on using Jordan's first name in order to protect his anonymity—a move that gets big laughs from the live studio audience. The show's premise supposes that Jordan will join Smalley in a daily affirmation despite the fact that he does not require any superficial emotional reinforcement. Smalley leads Jordan through a series of affirmations that end with Jordan repeating to himself: "All I have to do is be the best Michael I can be. Because I'm good enough, I'm smart enough, and doggone it, people like me" (Downey, 1991).

When Smalley asks, "Now, don't you feel better?" Jordan casually replies, "Well, I never really felt bad." Realizing he will have to detour from the pre-packaged script, Smalley replies glumly: "I am just a fool. I don't know what I'm doing. They're going to cancel the show. I'm going to die homeless and penniless and twenty pounds overweight, and no one will ever love me." Then, in a perfectly timed role reversal, Jordan steps in to counsel Smalley by offering the following: "Stuart, that's just not true. I think what you say on your show can be very helpful to people." Smalley replies, "You're right. It's just stinking thinking." After a brief hug, Smalley turns to the camera and says "I think this is the best show I've ever done. And you know what? I deserve it!" He turns to his mirror and ends with "Because I'm good enough, I'm smart enough, and doggonit, people like me!"

Now a large part of the humor here centers around the fact that Smalley has no idea how successful each of his (celebrity) guests is and, as a result, speaks to each one with a sort of painful obliviousness. It is this inside joke between the audience and guest star that gets the most laughs. However, for me—even at eleven years old—Smalley's hilarious appeal had more to do with the fact that it felt like he was poking fun at the Pollyanna-ish rhetoric and faux motivational language born out of something called the self-esteem movement that was being widely circulated throughout schools at the time and that was certainly prevalent in my own educational experience.

Bear with me here, because I don't intend this introduction to be taken solely as a collection of personal anecdotes but rather as an illustration of one of the first steps taken in the context of my efforts to contribute to the project of decolonizing interpretive research. In this initial stage—confronting my lived history/experience—the research process itself becomes an intimately experienced phenomenon that counters modernity's historical project of political and historical colonization. It requires, as Antonia Darder (2015) asserts, that researchers "grapple seriously with the struggle for our humanity, as Freire argued, in the face of hegemonic forces that seek to colonize every aspect of our lives, from birth to death" (p. 36), and demands that we critically interpret the ways in which we comprehend ourselves and make sense of the world.

I was part of that generational tidal wave of schoolchildren who rolled out of the 1980s and into the 1990s, an era when schools began to actively seek out updated self-esteem programs characterized by uncritical exercises such as encouraging children to write letters to themselves, telling themselves how special they are (Bergeron, 2016). As a result, I was witness to and often a reluctant participant in the classroom curricula and activities saturated with exercises to boost self-esteem as an end in itself—"Make a list of the ways in which you are special," "Let's all focus on Daniel, and each of us tell him what we admire about him, and so on" (Martin, 2014, p. 177). In my upper elementary and middle school years, when the self-esteem movement was perhaps at its zenith I was bombarded daily with countless examples demonstrating the different life paths that come as a result of having high versus low self-esteem. Is it any wonder then that upon reflection I would identify thematic parallels between my experience as a student in the classroom and the satirical representation of positive notions of self on display in "Daily Affirmation with Stuart Smalley"? I could sense even in my youth that the sketch was a robust critique of anyone who would earnestly use a phony term like "stinking thinking."

Undoubtedly, by the early 1990s, a nexus of policy makers and institutions had elevated self-esteem to the status of core beliefs—beliefs about the nature of self—that not only formed a basic component of an individual's common sense but was also dispatched as a supposed factor for success in the classroom and beyond. By this point self-esteem felt so common sense, so obvious, that we seldom thought to question its very validity (Bergeron, 2017). Meaningless mantras, like those espoused by Smalley on "Daily Affirmation," were being distributed to students in schools around the country by both specially trained "experts" and classroom teachers who were either consciously or unconsciously perpetuating a general ignorance of the self—especially as it pertains to subaltern students.

As a result,

> many working-class students of color are tossed into a frustrating and debili-
> tating dilemma: in order to be judged by their teachers—the majority of
> whom are white—as possessing high self-esteem they are expected to emulate
> hegemonic values and sensibilities foreign to their way of life.
>
> *(Darder, 2017, p. 8)*

This tension becomes even more apparent when we consider the number of studies that exist, which strongly challenge "the validity of the essentially monocultural criteria utilized in earlier studies to assess the self-concept/self-esteem of bicultural children" (Darder, 2015, p. 236). Yet, by the early 1990s, the self-esteem discourse and its associated programs had successfully infiltrated every aspect of our culture industry from media, to government, education, and so on and as such its primary aim was "to veil deeper political questions and ethical concerns that must be raised— questions and concerns that expose the hypocrisy and contradictions at work in the very fabric of American institutions and US democracy" (Darder, 2011, p. 3).

It was only once I reached graduate school that I came to realize that though the self-esteem mythos might seem strange to me, it is far from an alien concept or a harmless artifact of the emotional-intelligence complex. As the George Carlin (1990) epigraph that begins this chapter states, "Americans have a lot of trouble dealing with reality" and as a result have invented and disseminated a number of beliefs to hide their long histories of economic, social, and political oppression— forces and structures that give rise to inequalities and social exclusions. Schools, just like other institutions, hide behind a number of legitimating forms that exist to produce (and sustain) hegemonic ideologies.

For example, the talk on school campuses these days is dominated by jargon such as "implicit bias," "microaggressions," and "stereotype threats," which suggests that educators and students are starting to examine the structural inequalities that have undergirded the cultural hegemony of non-targeted groups (Euro-Americans) (Ber-geron, 2017). Buzzwords abound no less in education than in any other field of social interaction. As they gain popularity and slip into everyday speech, buzzwords assume the status of common sense. Consequently, the complexities surrounding their origins, applications, and intent are lost, and they become a representation of a most uncritical way to view reality. The self-esteem diaspora helped to place our experience in a vacuum by not properly acknowledging the problems of poverty, racism, sexism, and so on. Indeed, the tenets of the self-esteem discourse masquerade as though they could hold up under technical and empirical scrutiny, the culmination of some fully realized universal human trait. Yet, as my study came to show, in reality, these exist as ideas derivative of wider ideological, cultural, and political commitments.

Moreover, self-esteem has successfully replaced any vision of social empower-ment and self-determination with an insipid model of individual personal recovery (Bergeron, 2017). This model, enacted as a system of belief, has serious implications in a world where working-class children of color feel exponentially less valued and inferiorized by the dominant society, and where they continue to live mostly segregated by class and color and remain the cultural inspiration of phobia, stereotyping, anger, misunderstanding, and rejection.

> All of this takes place in concert with larger economic inequalities and hegemonic educational forces that hold firm a victim-blaming ideology of accountability and personal choice, along with the myth that equality and fair treatment is available to all deserving students who work hard.
>
> *(Darder, 2015, p. 31)*

My study focused on the range of commitments between the concept of self-esteem and the system of education. In order to appropriately address the impact of curricular interventions, particularly on oppressed communities, I employed a decolonizing interpretive methodology that "seeks to unveil and destabilize existing structures of power that perpetuate the material and social oppression of the most vulnerable populations" (Darder, 2015, p. 4). The proposal of an emancipatory and socially transformative agenda that is properly responsive to the demands of society seems a critical necessity, especially given the contemporary cultural climate dominated by calls to "Make America Great Again" (Bergeron, 2016).

A central occupation of my research focused on how self-esteem moved from a philosophical supposition to a hegemonic construct in mainstream Western culture; but I was primarily driven by the question of to what extent Western political and economic interests distort perceptions of the other, in order to preserve the classed, racialized, gendered, and sexual hierarchies or supremacies of Western cultural domination? Thus, the intention of my study was to critically investigate the implications of the myth of self-esteem. Crucial to this interrogation is an under-standing that what lies beyond any idealized notion of the self must ultimately be a critical understanding of one's individual and collective relationship to others and the world; and, moreover, that these relationships are fundamentally shaped by asymmetrical relations to power (Bergeron, 2016).

The primary aim of the scholarly work was decentering cultural notions or hege-monic beliefs of worth. Meaning it is at the same time a war on the historical and contemporary framework of value—especially the perceived worth of racialized, working-class bicultural students—and an assault on the values that serve to reinforce unequal relationships within spheres of culture and power (Darder, 2012a). Subaltern students are not just the victims of poverty and indifference but are also the victims of debilitating ideology, imposed on them by teachers and administrators who refuse to give up their ideas, even in the face of miserable results (Bergeron, 2016). Whatever the supposed value the concept of self-esteem may have had, it is now simply a tool that aids in deadening the emancipatory potential for education. Hence, we find ourselves today more deeply mired in Western ethnocentric notions of humanity where "individualism, object-based, future-focused, scientism, and materialism coun-teract the legitimacy of subordinate cultural community values and epistemological traditions of difference" (Darder, 2015, p. 35).

Decolonizing methodology

My scholarship is anchored to a decolonizing epistemological lens (Darder, 2018, 2015; Smith, 2012) focused on the experiences, concerns, impact, and outcomes of the use of the self-esteem construct on oppressed populations, through the system of education. As such, it begins with (and is in response to) Darder's (2002) extended critique of education "as a politicizing (or depoliticizing) institutional process that conditions students to subscribe to the prevailing social order" (p. 56) and her efforts to define a decolonizing interpretive methodology. The critical interpretive research design she proposes incorporates the decolonizing researcher as an unapologetically political participant, whose knowledge is understood as partial, unfinished, and deeply informed by the particular historical, economic, and cultural configurations of the times. As such, decolonizing interpretive design is meant to generate new insights or new theories from the richness of a detailed comparison of bodies of existing literature related to both theory and practice (Darder, 2015). This is essential if bicultural researchers are to disrupt and deliberately shift the hegemonic understanding of a social or educational phenomenon and move beyond hegemonic beliefs of schooling and society.

The present limitation of contemporary critical qualitative studies is that they "neglect to fully incorporate historical, cultural, philosophical, and educational literature as powerful socializing forces in the quest to dismantle oppressive notions of education" (Darder, 2015, p. 4). Decolonizing interpretive methodology is a way of integrating subaltern voices in the knowledge production of anti-colonial possibilities (Darder, 2018). In my work, this involved charting out a broad historical, political, and cultural analysis, in order to unveil the hegemonic structures of inequality that persists within schools and society (Darder, 2017). This process allows for a counterhegemonic form of thinking and reflecting upon the world essential to decolonizing interpretive research. Of this, Darder (2015) asserts:

> The underlying purpose of hegemonic power is to legitimate and conceal the imperial relations that today still undergird capitalism. As such the political work of the oppressed has always required the unveiling, naming, and challenging of asymmetrical relations of power and their consequences within schools, communities, and the larger society.
>
> *(p. 38)*

In order to critically initiate the decolonizing interpretive method, I would first have to confront my own worldview through engagement with scholarship like that of Freire (2000), whose work was as much about "unveiling the structures of domination as it was about decolonizing our minds of hegemonic ideologies that made us complicit with our oppression" (Darder, 2015, p. 4).

The fluidity and dynamism this interpretive framework encourages offered the space for me to engage with an enormous amount of anti-colonial literature. It is a rigorous process, but I don't use "rigor" in the traditional sense. According to

Darder (2018), academic rigor within the context of a decolonizing interpretive research design must be understood as:

> A deeply physical, emotional, and spiritual activity for bicultural researchers; which when practiced consistently, allows them to become more integral human beings, through a creative epistemological process of what Freire called problematization and radicalization (Darder, 2015)—an empowering process of knowledge construction that is also deeply rooted in the researcher's worldview.
>
> *(p. 9)*

Academic rigor in this sense allowed me to return to and incorporate the works of Fanon, Memmi, and Césaire, which came from my extensive study of Négritude as an undergraduate. Additionally, as an undergrad, I had the honor of learning from influential scholars such as Christopher A. McAuley, Otis Madison, and Cedric Robinson. Later, at Loyola Marymount I was further empowered through Darder's classroom teaching and mentorship, and the revolutionary scholarship of individuals like Giroux, Freire, Apple, hooks, and so on. It should be noted here that this decolonizing interpretive method also involves an investigation of curricula and curricular practices in order to expose what Henry Giroux (1981) describes as "those unstated norms, values, and beliefs embedded in and transmitted to students through underlying rules that structure the routines and social relationships in school and classroom life" (p. 385). This required analysis of much of the influential literature in the fields of education and psychology, in order to determine the different ways that self-esteem has been defined and conceptualized within education, and to trace how self-esteem moved from a philosophical supposition to a hegemonic construct in mainstream Western culture.

In this respect, demythologizing hegemonic beliefs is part of a larger process of empowerment—and innovative rethinking of interpretive research—in an effort to extend the analysis of a decolonizing methodology (Smith, 2012) to the construction of subaltern scholarship. Our efforts are aided by the simultaneous development of a dynamic and evolutionary understanding of knowledge as informed by the radicalization of consciousness—a revolutionary social process anchored in history and lived experience (Darder, 2018). As all of these elements blend together, the work becomes an embodied unification of the personal, professional, and political spheres.

Finally, Darder—a vigorous advocate for the intellectual nature of the work—also created practical circumstances that would support academic scholarship among a larger community. Within our graduate school cohort at Loyola Marymount University, Darder advised a small group of critical subaltern scholars who would work closely together—both academically and emotionally—to help meet projected deadlines but more than anything to struggle through the deeply personal work required of a decolonizing interpretive methodology. This small group, dubbed "The Bad-Bad News Bears" served, according to Nancy Fraser, as a subaltern counterpublic, or "arena where members of subordinate social groups invent and circulate counter discourses, which in turn permit them to formulate interpretations of their identities, interests, and needs" (cited in Darder, 2015, p. 70). The work of our particular subaltern counterpublic served to accelerate the development of a dynamic and evolutionary understanding of knowledge as informed by the radicalization of consciousness—a revolutionary social process anchored in the aforementioned lived experience and worldview of the researcher.

A healthy dose of dissidence

Admittedly, my engagement with the literature emanates from a position of dissident scholarship, an "oppositional interpretation born of the deep dialectical tension between hegemonic and subaltern knowledges that must be courageously navigated by the bicultural researcher" (Darder, 2011, p. 2). The question of standing up to power through dissident scholarship is central to the analysis of hegemonic educational notions such as self-esteem and the structural apparatus that sustains popular epistemic obedience to its ideological dictates (Darder, 2012b). It is difficult to dare to disobey, to say "no" to power because as Erich Fromm (2010) points out:

> Thus far throughout most of history a minority has ruled over the majority. This rule was made necessary by the fact that there was only enough of the good things of life for the few, and only the crumbs remained for the many. If the few wanted to enjoy the good things and, beyond that, to have the many serve them and work for them, one condition was necessary: the many had to learn obedience.
>
> *(pp. 9–10).*

Fromm's (2010) sentiments underscore the fact that dissident scholars must be constantly self-vigilant and prepared to defend against a variety of threats that, consciously or not, serve as effective roadblocks to the wider distribution of ideas (Darder, 2011). In my experience, these threats can vary in form; appearing as people who continue to insist that self-esteem is still hugely important or even fellow scholars who encourage a more quantitative-approach to research. Despite these attacks on my efforts—and remaining true to the ideals of a dissident scholar—I continue to be anchored instead to what Darder (2011) defines as "revolutionary possibilities that demand both intellectual discipline and irrepressible courage to speak the unspeakable, to stand alone if necessary, and to accept the material and emotional consequences of tramping over hegemony's 'holy ground and sacred cows'" (p. 2).

As such, bicultural (or subaltern) researchers understand that their work is part of a larger imperative for liberation. As my consciousness was radicalized through the process of my decolonizing interpretive labor, my awareness of the need to be ever vigilant of how political power in society is exercised became more apparent. In this context, it meant I had to bring my own history as a colonized subject to bear upon the manner in which I engaged philosophically, historically, and qualitatively with systematically linking the hegemonic belief in self-esteem to the larger apparatus of deficit thinking propagated within education and the larger society in terms of oppressed populations. In order to effectively navigate the demythologizing terrain of decolonizing interpretive research, I had to dialectically confront my own identity as a subaltern educator and researcher. This proved to be a pivotal and challenging step in the continued evolution of my study. Darder (2015) accurately describes this aspect of her decolonizing interpretive methodology as a meta-process that: "Involves the interrogation and disruption of currently held values, beliefs, and assumptions and from this systematic interrogation and disruption a move toward a bicultural reformulation of how the social phenomenon of oppressed populations is understood" (p. 4). My attempt, moreover, to deconstruct my own colonized or internalized epistemology—that for so much of my life had forced me into seeing the world from a dominant Western worldview—was further complicated by my subalternity within the dominant culture.

Freire wrote extensively on how the hegemonic culture of schooling socializes students to accept their conditioned place within the material order—determined by the colonizing forces and based on the political economy and structures of oppression (Darder, 2015, 2018). Samuel Bowles and Herbert Gintis (1976) echo this argument in *Schooling in Capitalist America*. Bowles and Gintis (1976) posit that the social hierarchy is not only maintained along divisions of cognitive skills, but also—and even more importantly—along noncognitive or behavioral skills that are directly related to social class. "These skills, which are differentially reinforced by different schools and among students in the same educational environments, are most significant in relation to what students learn about their appropriate future roles and social location within society" (Darder, 2012b, p. 6). However, as a Japanese-American student, teacher, and researcher, it has always felt like the system was unsure what to do with me, which is perhaps not surprising given that the lives of bicultural students comprise, for the most part, a disproportionately larger number of the disenfranchised.

As such, decolonizing scholarship challenges Eurocentric epistemologies, notions of identity, and Western colonizing concepts of human development (Smith, 2012). Given this phenomenon, Darder (2011) argues subaltern scholars are situated "in direct opposition to myths of modernity that would have us believe that our world can only be genuinely known through dispassionate inquiries and transcendent postures of scientific neutrality, as defined by Western philosophical assumptions of knowledge" (p. 1). Further, as Linda Tuhiwai Smith (2012) asserts, "The greater ideological significance of the myths, however, is that they support and give legitimacy to the role of conquest and migration in colonization" (p. 91) and the manner in which subaltern subjects, who are seen as not belonging, are defined. It is important then to challenge damaging myths and assumptions of identity, for how can scholars from subaltern communities ever let down our guard when we are subjected to a steady onslaught of questions about where our names are from or, because of how we appear, constantly being asked, "What are you?" In many ways, these frequent colonizing assaults to my subaltern existence left me seeking a more critical understanding of the self. For me, it emerged deeply through my decolonizing research efforts, culminating with the completion of my study.

Through engaging a decolonizing interpretive methodology, I also gained tremendous clarity in regards to my role as a bicultural educator, researcher, and educational leader. My scholarship went far beyond an intellectual exercise, but rather brought me to comprehend more deeply my own commitment to launching a substantiated critique of the axiomatic tenets of education, in order to create the counterhegemonic space for emancipatory practices to emerge—practices rooted in democratic cultural participation and political self-determination, especially within the context of historically oppressed communities in the United States. Further, the hope that underlies this methodology is that by critically analyzing dialectically the political and personal, subaltern researchers can create a place from which to think strategically about how to demythologize and combat the pervasive hegemonic beliefs that produce the racializing processes and limiting conditions tied to power, culture, and knowing, in our lives and in the larger society. Within the context of my study, this translated in my commitment to seek a substantiated critique of the cult of self-esteem, in order to create the space to explore new possibilities for emancipatory practices in oppressed communities—practices rooted in culturally democratic participation and political self-determination—with the ultimate purpose to contribute to transforming persistent colonizing structures of thought within education and society.

As alluded to earlier, the mainstream belief in self-esteem simultaneously pretends neutrality and universality. Accordingly, my decolonizing interpretive study concluded by asserting that it is necessary, now more than ever, to propose a socially transformative educational agenda, genuinely responsive to the liberatory needs of subaltern communities. In that as subaltern researchers contribute to demythologizing and recontextualizing notions of self and community, we can also more effectively intervene, through theory and practice, in ways that can effectively disrupt and shatter the culturally hegemonic force of debilitating beliefs such as self-esteem and their impact on our lives and the lives of our children.

Grounded in this humanizing emancipatory vision of decolonizing inquiry, my study critically interrogated the phenomenon of self-esteem and provided alternative readings that spoke to the problematic nature of self-esteem in contemporary curricular discourses, practices, and policies in education. In this way, my decolonizing interpretive study sought to offer new theoretical considerations to counter the oppressive ways mainstream teachers understand, speak to, and engage with students of color, as well as offer culturally democratic initiatives for their personal and collective empowerment. It is, therefore, through such a deliberate decolonizing approach to our subaltern analysis that questions tied to liberatory consciousness, social agency, and social empowerment undergird our theoretical and practical research efforts and our commitment to a more just world.

Note

1 This chapter is based on my doctoral dissertation research entitled *Esteemicide: Countering the Legacy of Self-Esteem in Education*. The study can be retrieved from https://pqdtopen. proquest.com/doc/1786971810.html?FMT=ABS.

References

Bergeron, K. E. (2016). *Esteemicide: Countering the legacy of self-esteem in education* (doctoral dissertation). Retrieved from https://pqdtopen.proquest.com/doc/1786971810.html?FMT=ABS.

Bergeron, K. (2017). *Challenging the cult of self-esteem in education: Education, psychology, and the subaltern self.* New York: Routledge.

Bowles, S., & Gintis, H. (1976). *Schooling in capitalist America: Educational reform and the contradictions of economic life.* New York: Basic Books.

Carlin, G. (Writer) (1990, June 2). In Urbisci, R. (Director/Producer), Doin' It Again [Television broadcast]. New York: HBO.

Darder, A. (2002). *Reinventing Paulo Freire: A pedagogy of love.* Boulder: Westview Press.

Darder, A. (2011, April 10). The making of a postcolonial dissident scholar. Speech presented at 2011 Postcolonial Studies in Education SIG Meeting American Educational Research Association Annual Meeting, New Orleans.

Darder, A. (2012a). *Culture and power in the classroom.* New York: Paradigm.

Darder, A. (2012b). Neoliberalism in the academic borderlands: An on-going struggle for equality and human rights. *Educational Studies* 48(5), 412–426.

Darder, A. (2015). Decolonizing interpretive research: A critical bicultural methodology for social change. *The International Education Journal: Comparative Perspectives* 14(2), 63–77.

Darder, A. (2017). Demythologizing self-esteem: Being our own example in the struggle for liberation. In K. Bergeron (Ed.), *Challenging the cult of self-esteem in education: Education, psychology, and the subaltern self.* New York: Routledge.

Darder, A. (2018). Decolonizing interpretive research: Subaltern sensibilities and the politics of voice. *Qualitative Research Journal* 18(2), 94–104.

Downey, J. (Writer). (1991, September 28). Season 17 Episode 1 [Television series episode]. Saturday Night Live. New York: NBC.

Freire, P. (2000). *Pedagogy of the oppressed.* New York: Bloomsbury Academic.

Fromm, E. (2010). *On disobedience: Why freedom means saying "no" to power.* New York: Harper.

Giroux, H. A. (1981). *Ideology, culture & the process of schooling.* Philadelphia: Temple University Press.

Martin, J. (2014). Psychologism, individualism and the limiting of the social context in educational psychology. In R. Corcoran (Ed.), *Psychology in education* (pp. 167–180). New York: Springer.

Smith, L. T. (2012). *Decolonizing methodologies* (2nd edition). London: Zed Books.

5

EPISTEMOLOGICAL DISRUPTIONS[1]

Bibinaz Pirayesh

> To rupture is to break from previously established ways of knowing. It is to trouble what is taken for granted, to reimagine the nature and scope of knowledge. When we speak of rupture, we are speaking of epistemological shifts—reinscribing what knowledge is, how it can be acquired, and the extent to which knowledge pertinent to any given subject informs concepts such as community, morality, politics, and identity.
>
> *(Kingsmith, 2017)*

I came to my study almost in secret. It was as if I had been hiding a deep truth within myself for the entire course of my academic formation; a secret I didn't dare speak as I pursued a Bachelor's degree in neuroscience and a Master's later in psychology. But a secret that remained close to my heart. My secret was reflected in the uneasy feeling that despite all my successes in school, none of it felt true or grounded in what I have experienced as an educational therapist. Then, at the start of a doctoral program—another great marker in the Western academic tradition—I found myself feeling uneasy and conflicted once more. How could I pursue a degree and study a problem of practice in my field when I knew that the problems I saw were rooted in the very institution attempting to solve them? After a decade of work assisting children with learning struggles navigate institutions of schooling that were constructed to label and exclude them, what problem could I possibly study other than the problem of the field itself?

Mind, Brain, and Education (MBE), along with Neuroscience and Education, which theoretically inform the practice of educational therapy, continue to offer an easy answer: education, and more specifically special education, needs to become more rigorous and scientific. Science, psychology, and now the study of the brain, has and will continue to discover and create the necessary tools to diagnose and "fix" the ways in which the brains of my students deviated from the norm and educators have only to understand and adopt these tools and modernize their practice in order to rescue failing children. This was the great promise of my field, and my secret was, I didn't buy it.

What my experiences as an educational therapist had taught me was that it was connection, love, trust, hope, and feeling safe, that nurtured brains and alleviated "disorders," given that disordered brains are often better understood as symptoms of disconnection or social alienation (Mate, 2000, 2011). My work with communities, in fact, had taught me that it is human values supportive of families, parents, and schools that make the difference. An hour of uninterrupted loving human attention does more for a child than three months of a brain training app. Similarly, the presence of a supportive advocate does more in supporting a family or teacher to assist a student who is struggling academically than a hundred tests, evaluations, or educational plans. This I had come to know through lived experience. So, while I came into my doctoral program hoping to study and understand how to scale my work as an educational therapist so that all students, not just a select few who could afford it, might benefit from advances in neuroscience and education, the quiet secret I carried was, how do you scale love?

My field seemed oblivious to this question. Instead, there existed a binary between neuroscience and education, scientist and educator; a kind of imagined or fabricated expert conflict that was perpetuated by an abstracted, pseudo-harmonious ideology that reproduced and exacerbated the problems in the field. As an immigrant and bicultural researcher, I knew such setups only too well and the message I had received repeatedly was that there was no rising above or integrating of the poles. What there was, is, and always will be, is a creative epistemological tension that can serve as the ground for all learning and growth. To say teachers and scientists are different then is a falsehood, because they are both human and it is through dialogue that I came to believe that we would find new answers by asking better questions. But how would I get there? How would I study this phenomenon steeped in oppressive conditions of professional elitism and hierarchy utilizing a traditional empirical methodology, when the methodology I needed had to be born from the very human sensibilities of the colonized that the field failed to acknowledge?

So began my ethnographic journey into a decolonizing interpretive methodology and the realization that if I wanted to finally engage my secret question, I needed to find a different set of tools and a different language by which to frame my research. This, however, was a petrifying thought. I had been socialized, conditioned, and well-trained in the scientific method since elementary school. This was the gold standard of knowledge construction. How could I be working toward a doctoral degree, in the very system rooted in an oppressive epistemology, while questioning it? As I commenced in the unknown terrain of a decolonizing methodology, I felt not just like a fraud, but an enemy of the state. As if even questioning the method itself was an act of treason. But soon I came to recognize that this is, indeed, a first requirement of an interpretive decolonizing methodology: the willingness to engage with "the politics of voice" (Darder, 2018, p. 1) and, by so doing, coming to realize that *the subaltern can speak* (Spivak, 1988).

Yet, initially, I wasn't sure I could find my voice; and even after wrestling with this question and deciding to consider and embrace the possible wisdom in my own experience, I was still up against the hardwiring of my thinking. I was in need of a clear path for I truly had no idea where I was going, nor was I prepared to venture into the unknown epistemological terrain of a different way of knowing. I had no clear method, no steps to follow, or formula to apply. I was thrust into the unknown with nothing to hold on to; and although I kept reminding myself of Freire's (1998) invitation to be "open to risk [and] the adventure of the spirit" (p. 102), I found it difficult in my own mind to move confidently beyond the Western epistemological tradition that had colonized my thinking.

So, my fears fought me hard. I would say that in the first year of this research, I spent more time wrestling with the idea of a decolonizing methodology trying to get it to kneel to traditional research methods, in order to make my study and myself conform ideologically, than actually embracing the method itself. But, the fact is, this is a large aspect of the work for any subaltern researcher committed to disrupting colonizing ideologies. I had to learn to let go and trust the creative tension within myself, allowing the process to lead me wherever it might, based on nothing more than a conviction that we all have a right to struggle to understand the truths of our conditions. Soon, I also came to understand that this is the very ethics of liberation that informs the power of a decolonizing methodology.

It took a long time, but slowly there emerged in my struggle the room for a more fluid understanding of the difference that had been at work in my life and practice all along. But this came only after a full acknowledgment of the trauma of the epistemic violence of Western thinking that had been perpetrated both on my own individual psyche, and on the psyche of those who protected the field. Hence, I came to realize that in order for MBE to move forward, it too needed to undergo a decolonization process and to be re-interpreted theoretically by the very people engaged in its work. In this way, I came to know that my own empowerment as a practitioner in the field was inextricably linked to a systematic political effort to shift the field in both theory and practice. In short, it was the power and "authority of lived experience" (hooks, 1994) as a decolonizing interpretive researcher that gave me new insights into my study. It was through this deeply physical, emotional, and spiritual activity, and in becoming a more integral human being, that I became empowered to problematize and radicalize my work as a subaltern researcher.

So, while tracing and naming the ideological roots of the field is an integral part of a decolonizing interpretive methodology, this process is also about addressing our own conditioned fears and, as a subaltern researcher, embracing the right to challenge the tradition of my field of study. In many ways, this process informed the initial dimensions of my research, where I traced the history and epistemological roots of neuroscience, its move into education, and ultimately the morphing into the current vision of MBE to make education more "scientific." I cannot stress the difficulty I underwent in making this paradigmatic shift, so I could question effectively the normalized assumptions that seek to make education more scientific and the problematics of mainstream notions of evidence-based research.

I quickly came to understand that to move toward a decolonizing lens and show that another way was possible, I had to understand the literature and the history; I needed to comprehend how deeply detrimental the "myth of modernity" had been to the field and to the children supposedly being served. This to say that my search and review of the literature, my engagement with the history of the field, my exploration into the politics of epistemologies, and challenging the consequences of MBE ideologies grounded in the Western scientific paradigm head on was therefore as important a part of my own decolonization process as the challenges my research posited to the oppressive ideological configurations of my field of study. So in this regard, a decolonizing interpretive research process deeply embodies the method itself at the personal, academic, and political levels of the work.

My own experience in utilizing a decolonizing interpretive methodology affirmed Freire's (1985) notion: "the act of study, in sum, is an attitude toward the world" that "reflects its author's confrontation with the world" (p. 3). As such, I had to confront the colonizing nature of the field, just as I had to confront my own colonized thinking. This speaks to the true dialectic process of a decolonizing methodology and it was then in understanding and questioning the very tools and lens we use to name and process the world that I came to finally face my big secret and ask: How can we create a decolonizing practice of MBE that genuinely engages the needs of all children in the process of their own education, emancipation, and humanity?

Decolonizing epistemologies

At the heart of decolonizing epistemologies is an understanding that within the Western paradigm of science and education, indigenous knowledge has been systematically excluded by curricular impositions of "official" knowledge (Smith, 1999) and thus must be challenged, denounced, and transformed. My deep dive into the history of neuroscience and the epistemological formations of the American educational system by the sciences revealed not only the colonial roots of MBE but served as a warning, sounding an alarm for the potentially destructive consequences MBE can have on education and our children today, if not re-imagined. This called for a liberatory ethics embraced by Freire (2000, 1998), Smith (1999), Santos (2005), Paraskeva (2011, 2016), and Darder (2017), who argue that the struggle for social justice must challenge the *coloniality of power* at the very foundations of Eurocentric knowledge.

The key problem that was revealed, as I began to undertake my research in critically examining the literature, the language of the field, its authors and researchers and explanations given for the enduring divide, was that the oppressive nature of Eurocentric research designs were not only due to epistemological differences, but rather to the subordinating politics that created these differences, resulting in asymmetrical relations of power. Moreover, there is an absence of a critical lens in the field that could potentially shed new light in how we interrogate MBE's potential for just interventions in supporting liberatory classroom practices for co-creating knowledge and establishing horizontal structures and conditions for dialogical praxis. In other words, what decolonizing interpretive methodology allowed me to do from the beginning was to recognize that the very question and problem identified in the field needed to be shaped by subaltern sensibilities—that is from the worldview of those being colonized by traditional practices of education. The gap between research and practice and between neuroscience and education then was not a gap, but a symptom of an abyssal divide (Santos, 2005).

This "misdiagnosis" in the field has had harrowing consequences. As special education, for example, continues to fall short of its aims to serve students in public schools (Connor et al., 2008; Dudley-Marling & Burns, 2014; Smith et al., 2009) and new brain research tied to cognition and learning is gaining traction in educational curriculum (Fischer et al., 2010), the absolute nature of scientific research is propped up by fields like MBE as the new *great white hope*—the new answer to all our problems, even as history shows that science in education has always advanced some children, while labeling and leaving most behind others (Four Arrows et al., 2009). What my decolonizing research assisted me to show is that emancipatory efforts to bring brain research into educational settings must therefore contend forthrightly with the long history of the colonizing manifestation of scientific research within the mainstream (Darder, 2012; Smith, 1999; Gould, 1996).

Yet, in the discussion of these issues, the ideological rhetoric within the fields of neuroscience and education, including inclusion and equity rhetoric, continue to embrace the myth of neutrality and objectivity in the name of science, denying the very political nature of their underlying mission. What is even more alarming is that some of the literature in the field suggests that many of its contributing scholars remain unaware of how disconnected and disconnecting their scientific approach remains. Even within discussions of the historical and philosophical differences between science and education, there is no discussion related to the historicity or ideological dimensions of knowledge, which, as part of the critical tradition, reminds us that knowledge is created within historical, cultural, political and economic contexts and, thus, all knowledge must be situated in history and the social order (Darder, 2014, 2015). In short, what my work helped to illuminate was that the lack of a critical lens in the field is itself problematic, in that it contributes to the ongoing colonizing distortions at work within MBE. It was through using a decolonizing interpretive methodology that I was able to begin to uncover the dominant ideologies (in this case within science) that are normalized as neutral and, from there, begin to chip away at the preconditioned and hegemonic patterns in how we make sense of the MBE universe.

Disrupting the logic of MBE

As new brain technologies forge a revolution (Four Arrows et al., 2009), the evolving influence of the MBE movement serves as a testament to an increasing interest in brain sciences within education, which gives rise to the need to remain vigilant of the limiting and narrow logic at work in both academia and scientific research, particularly with respect to issues of implementation within public education. In the MBE literature, however, most educators are generally seen as the problem, in that they are not considered scientific enough and, thus, must be further schooled in the ways of science. In order to sift through the impact of this phenomenon, a decolonizing methodology demands that the subaltern researcher put him or herself at the center of the work. As an educator, and more specifically, a bicultural[2] educator, I soon began to see that it would be my bicultural voice (Darder, 2012) and subaltern sensibilities that could challenge the hegemonic values of MBE; in that, as Four Arrows et al. (2009) argue, "Western neuroscientists and the philosophers who attempt to make sense of their 'objective' findings may lead us further away from, not closer to, the truth about what humans can do to live in harmony on this planet" (p. vii).

It was, then, in beginning with my own positionality as a subaltern researcher, by honoring my own unique bicultural perspective, that I was eventually able to identify the lack of critical literature in MBE as a problem that places the field at risk of, first, not being able to have the impact it seeks, and, second, perhaps even more problematic, reproducing bias and exclusionary outcomes that widen the exclusionary divide. Hence, it was in examining the problematic history of the field using a decolonizing interpretive methodology that I began to ask: What types of theoretical reformulations and new pedagogical practices are required within the field of MBE, if issues of social justice are to be central to research, teaching, and practice?

A fundamental epistemological shift in the very questions and productions of knowledge in the field was, therefore, necessary in order to move forward. This shift would need to be tectonic so as to provoke revolutionary thinking about the very knowledge of the field and how to decolonize it. This epistemological disruption at the very root of the field was then the only possible decolonizing response, given the abyssal divide I had discovered in my examination of the history and epistemological tenets of the field, and so, once again, I found myself anchoring my work upon a decolonizing interpretive methodology, but now evolving in my engagement in a way that formidably countered the traditional scientific methodologies of my earlier intellectual formation.

In conducting my study, disrupting dominant epistemologies and struggling against epistemicides required, as Paraskeva (2011, 2016) argues, both *a de-territorialized approach* and *a critical itinerant position*. This fundamentally proposes that we can move beyond the legitimating logic of the Western epistemological platform, which is rooted in honoring one's subaltern positionality, which is at the root of a decolonizing methodology. Repeatedly returning to a recognition that there is no one cohesive or universal representation or authoritative voice that informs this critical methodology (Darder, 2014) and that we can only rely on liberatory principles rather than a linear road map, slowly allowed me to envision my own itinerant vision in response to my research question. I came to see that, just as I was mobilized away from a colonizing ethos of knowledge production, MBE needed to move away from its dominant territorialized curricular wars—predicated on a positivist epistemology of supremacy—and fixed knowledge borders toward epistemological diversity, itinerant fluidity, and socio and cognitive justice (Paraskeva, 2011, 2016).

So, if epistemology is defined as the study of knowledge, its sources, structures, and borders, and how knowledge gets created, justified, disseminated, and legitimized, an epistemological disruption means re-reading and re-inventing the dominant discourse. But epistemology is also concerned with how our knowledge of reality is essentially limited by the means and methods used to discern what is viewed as legitimate knowledge. And, as the previous discussion demonstrates, MBE knowledge is also implicated not just by the scientific method but the dominant system of schooling, where hegemonic ways of knowing and knowledge production are embedded and reinforced across disciplines and within the larger context of society.

The coloniality of power

Engaging with the coloniality of power is a central construct of epistemological disruption within the context of decolonizing interpretive methodology. Important to this discussion, as noted earlier, is that science's epistemology is not just about the promotion of positivist epistemologies, but rather about the consolidation of power. The Western scientific method, in fact, has achieved what Haraway (1988) argues is the "god trick of seeing everything from nowhere" (p. 581). From this vantage point, hegemonic epistemology has been able to violently impose forms of oppressive knowledge production directly linked to the persistence of the coloniality of power (Quijano, 2000). In other words, what my study consistently showed is that MBE as a field needs to contend with its epistemological aim, which is to colonize education (in the interest of the status quo) through its scientific method, all in the name of advancement and progress. Central to this debate then is not simply the fields of science or education, but larger structures and relationships of power that are conserved by the coloniality of power and its control over knowledge production.

Boaventura de Sousa Santos (2005, 2007c) has argued that an *abyssal line* divides the hegemonic epistemological terrain—a line that depicts the global South as non-existent. Consequently, this produces deadening epistemologies or epistemicidal knowledge that bolster the unequal power dynamics necessary for the hegemonic production and containment of this non-existence (Janson & Paraskeva, 2015). This one-dimensional consciousness, so to speak, is anchored in a politics of "epistemicide," that is, the extermination of knowledge and ways of knowing that coincide with the emergence of modern colonial structures of knowledge, as the foundational epistemology of Westernized systems of governance and education (Santos, 2007c).

Thus, it is not just that the scientific epistemology is limiting, but that what science (steeped in epistemicidal values) has managed to do is to kill off other ways of knowing (Smith, 1999). What this signals here is the coloniality of power, a phenomenon linked to the practices and persistent legacies of European colonialism within both governing social orders, as well as the production of knowledge (Quijano, 2000). Here, non-Western ways of knowing are absorbed, invisibilized, or destroyed (Santos, 2007a, 2007c) by the abiding sensibilities and epistemologies of the hegemonic order (Darder, 2018) such that "the model of power that is globally hegemonic today presupposes an element of coloniality" (Quijano, 2000, p. 533).

As such, epistemicidal knowledge has devastating effects globally—in sync with a global coloniality of power (Grosfoguel, 2011; Mignolo, 2007; Quijano, 2000)—that has resulted in internationalized forms of cognitive injustice, which have supported attacks upon the very existence of racialized populations who exist outside of the global North (Santos, 2007b). As Paraskeva (2011) argues, "the epistemicide needs to be seen as a world *tout court* Western secular rationality spreading from the hard sciences to the social sciences and on to the humanities," such that the humanities are "gradually being dominated by the prestigious Anglophone discourses (and practices), due no doubt to its associations with the power structures of modernity (slavery, eugenics, technology, industry, and capitalism) that impose a positivist worldview" (p. 3).

My decolonizing interpretive study also led me to engage the colonizing question of language, with respect to my critical analysis of MBE and, in particular, my concern about why the field struggles with a language of identity and unity (Knox, 2016; Scott & Curran, 2010). Samuels (2009) matter-of-factly states, "Historically, science and education have demonstrated separate, but interwoven, influences on society that have led to a characterization of science as prestigious and education as failure ridden" (p. 46). This language, though it is meant to "help," is not only insulting, it reproduces traditional beliefs about education and educators that are simply not true, reflecting a version of history where one group is superior over the other and where science reigns supreme (Smith, 1999).

Similarly, the linguistic supremacy attributed to the prefix "neuro" and the discourse that follows it is itself problematic. The use of this prefix, like the use of brain images, immediately extends commonsensical legitimacy, while at the same time undermining other forms of knowledge. The word exemplifies the colonizing language of power (Rizvi et al., 2006), "being circulated, not in any neutral way but on the basis of a politically sanctioned authority" (Billington, 2017, p. 868), gaining an ever-expanding sphere of influence (Rose, 2006; Kirmayer, 2012). The fact is, "renaming teaching as 'brain-based education', while keeping the present model in place, is like rearranging the deck chairs on the Titanic" (Cozolino, 2013). If MBE is to be a true transdisciplinary field, my research insists that it must be "resistant to a universalizing language – a language of empirical inquiry that has often been anchored to dominant epistemologies" (Darder, 2015, p. 63) and, thus, has perpetuated the coloniality of power within the hegemonic apparatus of education, science, and knowledge production.

The hegemony of education, science, and knowledge

No hegemonic apparatus has been employed more completely as a global tool for the control of knowledge than the Western educational system. What is of note here is that, at the end of the nineteenth century, the paradigm too went through an epistemological shift where the metaphor of "the mind as a muscle" (Paraskeva, 2011, p. 22) began to impose a new social order within the United States via a mainstream curriculum where only institutionally authorized knowledge was to be introduced in schools. This move, which further solidified the culture of positivism (Giroux, 1981), was fundamentally concerned "with controlling and dominating the natural and human environment" (Wexler, 1976, p. 8), thus fostering cognitive passivity (Kincheloe, 1993) through a colonizing curriculum built on a persistent legacy of genocide with respect to all other knowledge forms.

A dark chapter in the history of American education—and not limited to the United States but extending globally to all colonizing empires of the West—includes the outlawing of indigenous languages and cultures and the forced removal of indigenous children from their families and cultures, in order for them to be "educated" in "modern" schools by Western (superior) thinking (Smith, 1999) educators. No place is the politics of location (Braidotti, 2013; Haraway, 1988) then more relevant than in the classroom, where the battle over knowledge is played out by educators and where the dominion of science is presented as an authorizing corpus of knowledge, without being analyzed with respect to its perpetuation of cognitive and social exclusions. As Freire (in Freire & Macedo, 1987) argued, *naming the world* is directly linked to claiming it and to claiming those ways of seeing the world that count as legitimate within the context of lived experiences—this speaks, in particular, to the knowledge that has been systematically excluded and erased from the educational process of subaltern populations (Darder, 2012, 2017).

In short, what is needed in MBE is not a new and more sophisticated scientific educational curriculum but a disruption of the very epistemology of the field that goes beyond the struggle for curriculum relevance and beyond the tensions between science and education, as described in the MBE literature, in order to assume a more itinerant approach (Paraskeva, 2011). Here, cognitive fluidity and non-fixity drive the struggle for curriculum relevance away from knowledge epistemicides and toward a more emancipatory and just path. The epistemological disruption essential to a decolonizing methodology, moreover, can and must be present in any study with an underlying transformative intent.

In the specific case of MBE, however, what was of particular concern was the manner in which science's epistemicides have colonized schooling and society as a whole in such a way that it has forced education as a field to also be absorbed into its epistemology, thus rendering invisible all other traditions and identities, in the name of science and modernity. What has emerged is an Orwellian reality that has been both naturalized and normalized as commonsense and embedded into the hidden curriculum of hegemonic schooling (Darder, 2012). About this, Michael Apple (1990) noted that the hidden curriculum consists of "the norms and values that are implicitly, but effectively, taught in schools and that are not usually talked about" (p. 84). Simple examples are embedded in the deeply psychologized premises of American education: (1) that the aim of life is happiness, that is maximum pleasure; and (2) that egotism, selfishness, and greed, as the system needs to generate them in order to function, actually lead to harmony and peace (Fromm, 1976). Similarly are widespread proclamations of self-esteem within American education rooted in quasi-scientific explanations that belie the underlying conditioned passivity of hegemonic schooling, particularly with respect to racialized and impoverished communities (Bergeron, 2017).

Unfortunately, these deceptive notions are also the basis for the failure of the "Great Promise" of education in the United States (Paraskeva, 2011) and are implicated in the hidden curriculum, which Ivan Illich (1971) argues, "adds prejudice and guilt to the discrimination which a society practices against some of its members and compounds the privilege of others with a new title to condescend to the majority" (p. 33). It is part of the bureaucratic and managerial functions of the school and serves as a place and ritual of initiation into a consumer society obsessed with the aims of science to explain, to conquer, to perfect, to demystify, and to control working populations (Illich, 1971). Perhaps this is why scholars who identify themselves as critical neuroscientists—who are concerned with the tremendous pace of developments in neuroscience and an increasing emphasis on using these findings to impact the cultural and the social lives of human beings—push back against the hegemonic curriculum of the field (Choudhury & Slaby, 2011) and its relationship to the economy. But how has Western epistemology, in concert with the kind of big business that comes at the expense of humanity (Paraskeva, 2011, 2016; Steiner et al., 2004), shaped MBE and how does this need to shift?

As Paraskeva (2011) argues, an accurate examination of the nature of conflict enables one to explicitly experience the profoundly political nature of curriculum content, unveiling the overt and intricate nexus between the hidden curriculum and the knowledge relayed via school dynamics. Since social change and progress emerge and are fueled by the dynamics of conflict, these dynamics cannot be dissociated from the curriculum as a mechanism of knowledge construction. With such dissociation, "there [will be] no union between the school and society" (Gramsci, 1971, p. 35). In short, any decolonizing educational analysis must take into account the asymmetrical power dynamics that inform the pedagogical culture and political vision of the educational process within and outside schools.

The conflict between neuroscience and education must thus be viewed from different perspectives and should be understood as a key dialectical moment for engaging the dynamics of legitimization and potential emancipatory possibilities. This occurs through decolonizing interrogations put forth by this critical interpretive methodology, which questions who is and who is not part of the conversation and why. What issues sit at the core of the conversation? Where are the voices of teachers and students? What is the impact of the conversation on classroom practice? Who benefits from the "complicated" conversation? And in which language(s) are educational conversations to be carried out? It is by way of such interrogations of limits and conflicts within the field that the potential is found to challenge epistemicides. Once it is understood that education is itself a positivist enterprise drowning under a crisis of curriculum and a call for reform, which stems not from a lack of "empirical evidence" in the field, as MBE suggests, but rather from the intransigent presence of the positivist tradition, possibilities for transformative interventions can evolve organically in response to humanizing questions focused on the grounded well-being of students' lives.

However, to carry out a transformative approach, Paraskeva (2011) reminds us that, for example, when dealing with conflicts in curriculum and epistemology, we must remain cognizant that to theorize a new field and a new curriculum—in this case for MBE—requires we:

> (1) put into historical context the emergence and development of the history of the field; (2) unveil the emergence of a group of critical theorists within the curriculum field; (3) offer a new metaphor of the field as "a critical curriculum river" that meanders extensively to help understand these theorists' complex journey, including the battles fought for control of the field; and (4) examine and lay out a critique of the reconceptualist movement.
>
> *(p. 1)*

By so doing, there is a possibility of MBE emerging as a reinvented field, not anchored in any one discipline or in the positivist epistemology that has ruled education over its history, but rather as an itinerant field that encompasses a rhizomic view of "ands" instead of "ors" (De Freitas, 2012; Strom, 2015) and, therefore, supports a theory and practice of greater inclusiveness in the process.

Examples of epistemological disruptions

There is no question that conflict in the field of MBE reflects the larger societal and ideological conflicts at work in a society where both scientific and educational formations reinforce and reproduce forms of social exclusions. MBE will forever be plagued by this conflict, so long as we refuse to look at and disrupt the underlying epistemological formations that reproduce particular forms of inequalities inherent in the field. With this mind, the following provides a brief discussion of several examples of epistemological disruptions that surfaced in my study by utilizing a decolonizing interpretive lens in examining the field of MBE.

Disrupting the medicalization of education

Claiming that "every major modern business grounds itself solidly in research that is shaped by practical questions about how products function and how they can be used effectively in context" (Fischer, 2009, p. 3), MBE posits itself as the scientific and business solution to the problems of education. Oblivious to the history of science in education, as well as previous catastrophic attempts to "fix" education using both scientific and business models, MBE forges on, with the call for a *new science* (Fischer et al., 2007) to save education from its humanistic peril. Even more ironic, the comparison between medical research and medical practice is used to argue that research must move beyond the ivory tower and into the classroom arena of "real" life, in order to ensure that educational practices are made "available for scientific scrutiny" (Fischer et al., 2007, p. 1). While there was no examination within the literature of whether such a comparison could or should be made, the commonsensical language of interweaving and reciprocity between the medical and educational fields peppers the literature throughout.

Hence, comparisons between science and education are then used to make the case that "Knowledge and evidence-based approaches to education put forward the fact that educational systems are inadequate to provide an answer to the challenges of the 21st century" (Pasquinelli, 2011, p. 186), making the expert claim that scientific principles should guide education, rather than intuition or professional wisdom. From a decolonizing reading of the literature, it seems the argument is that educational practice and policy must be medicalized; that is, it must be based on scientifically sanctioned empirical evidence, as the time has come for "education, biology, and cognitive science, to join together to create a new science and practice of learning and development" (Fischer et al., 2007, p. 1). Linked to the same hegemonic epistemology that legitimizes this imperative, the US Department of Education's 2002 Strategic Plan set a specific goal to transform education into an evidence-based field and to increase the relevance of research to meet practitioners' needs, asserting:

> unlike medicine, agriculture and industrial production, the field of education operates largely on the basis of ideology and professional consensus. As such, it is subject to fads and is incapable of the cumulative progress that follows from the application of the scientific method and from the systematic collection and use of objective information in policy making.
>
> *(US Department of Education, Office of the Deputy Secretary, 2002)*

Moreover, what the argument for this scientification of education in MBE essentially does is to reinforce, bolster, and enact abyssal thinking. Of this Santos (2007c) argues:

> Modern Western thinking is an abyssal thinking. It is a system of visible and invisible distinctions, and the invisible sustain the visible. The invisible distinctions are established through radical lines that divide social reality into two distinctive realms: the universe from this side of the line and the universe of the other side of the line. The division is such that the other side of the line vanishes as reality, becomes nonexistent and is simultaneously produced as nonexistent. Everything that is produced as nonexistent is radically excluded for it lies beyond the realm of what the accepted conception of inclusion considers to be its other.
>
> *(p. 23)*

Given the history of science in education in the past, it is not difficult to imagine a future where classroom teachers are expected to use neuroscience methods as the scientific and academic pillar from which to "diagnose" normalcy on one side of the divide, making everyone on the other side simply irrelevant or non-existent—in the process solidifying the medicalization of education.

Furthermore, once neuroscience rules supreme, fighting for the inclusion of children who are "othered" or advocating for inclusionary practices where diversity and difference are not viewed through the dichotomous black-and-white lens of science becomes increasingly more difficult. This is especially true, given that "epistemological disenfranchisement" (Connell, 2007, p. 109) is not limited to MBE. In education itself, despite disruptions in the 1960s and 1970s (Bowles & Gintis, 2011; Henry, 1963; Jackson, 1968; Jencks, 1972; Kozol, 1967) that for a moment inflamed the US curriculum field (Paraskeva, 2011, 2016), what persists is a culture of high risk testing (Darder, 2012, 2017), now being intensified by a push for "the shaping of individual brains via targeted practices in the classroom" (Szűcs & Goswami, 2007, p. 120), which is quickly becoming the new definition of learning in schools today. All this is happening alongside the simultaneous demand for scientific evidence-based policy-making (Alberts, 2010), which has become increasingly more vociferous in the last three decades.

Researchers who promote pushing neuroscience, with its medicalized under-pinnings, into education argue that "the objective of evidence-based education at this level is to ensure that future research on education meets the criteria of scientific validity, high-quality, and practical relevance that is sometimes lacking in existing evidence on educational activities, processes, and outcomes" (Davies, 1999, p. 109). Such a reductive analysis, however, ignores the relational and more encompassing vision of democratic education, by failing to recognize the current need for resistance to and transformation of injustice within schools and society. Moreover, the science offered by brain images today may not only be misleading but could be in danger of crudely repeating old mistakes. Of this, Bao and Pöppel (2012) argue, "An uncritical use of new imaging technology may open the door to a new kind of old fashioned phrenology" (p. 2144). Even if the images and "evidence" offered by neuroscience might not be misleading in and of themselves, their inclusion in education without critical preparation and engagement of what these mean and their varied impact "merely enhance the processes and procedures of psychopathologisation" (Billington, 2017, p. 875).

Disrupting neuromyths

Another major area of concern for scholars in MBE is the issue of neuromyths. The creation of these "biased distortions of scientific fact" (Howard-Jones, 2014, p. 1) are generally blamed by those in the field on educators and/or lay people who are not trained in the sciences and perpetuate myths because of their ignorance. In article after article of *The Journal of Mind, Brain, and Education*, there are references to the dangers of neuromyths and the importance of guiding against them

(Christoff, 2008; Grotzer, 2011; Lindell & Kidd, 2013; Pasquinelli, 2012; Tardif et al., 2015), as well as on the importance of "Educating to Use Evidence in Thinking About Education" (Newcombe, 2013, p. 147). Ironically, the tendency toward reductionism is highlighted in the discourse around neuromyths in the field, but without any discussion of the reductionist tendencies of science itself.

According to Vandana Shiva (1993), modern Western patriarchy's epistemological tradition is reductionistic. This is because it not only "reduces the capacity of humans to know nature both by excluding other knowers and other ways of knowing, but also because it manipulates science as inert and fragmented matter" (p. 22). In a way, such a reductionist mechanism is "protected not merely by its own mythology, but it is also protected by the interests it serves. Far from being an epistemological accident, reductionism is a response to the needs of a particular form of economic and political organization" (p. 23). The mechanical reductionist Western scientific paradigm, Shiva argues, together with "the industrial revolution and the capitalist economy are the philosophical, technological and economic components of the same process" (p. 24).

But, as was made evident in my study, the trouble with neuromyths is not just that "the cognitive and brain sciences have been misunderstood, and misused" (Pasquinelli, 2012, p. 89); or that "there are many hypotheses in science which are wrong" (Sagan cited in Pasquinelli, 2012, p. 89)—but rather why this is so? In trying to understand this phenomenon, a variety of compounding questions surfaced for examination. Why does scientific information, even wrong scientific information, feed into "neuro-phillia" (Pasquinelli, 2012, p. 91)? Are the reasons limited to the untrained mind of educators and the general public, or the communication shortcomings of the media as the literature in MBE suggests? Or is there something deeper going on? Are the dangers of the persistence of neuromyths and the appetite for brain news simply due to "deeper cognitive intuitions" (p. 89) that favor confirmation of bias or the tendency to seek or interpret fresh information in a way that confirms previous beliefs (Nickerson, 1998) limited by unfounded notions of hemispheric specialization? Or does neuroscience promise to confirm our hidden desires for power? Can MBE truly protect itself from the rise and dangers of "neuromarketing" (Lindell & Kidd, 2013, p. 35) and "the seductive allure of neuroscience explanations" (Weisberg et al., 2015, p. 429) without asking why it is that "by implying a strong scientific basis, 'brain-based' product names are remarkably effective in implicitly manipulating consumer opinion" (Lindell & Kidd, 2013, p. 35). In other words, how can the field of MBE critique and counter its engrained exclusionary beliefs?

What became most apparent here was that when we leave out issues related to power and exclusions within the history of science and education in this country, we also close off the possibility for "openly discussing disciplinary differences and assumptions" (Fischer & Daniel, 2009, p. 2). How can we, therefore, critique neuromyths and the dangers of the brain-hype without a deeper interrogation into the epistemological roots that inform them and how the field promotes these neuromyths for its own economic and political interests? If MBE aims to inform education in an increasingly global world, it cannot do so without "remapping the order of knowing" (Mignolo, 2011, p. 77) and addressing the contradictions inherent in its formations—an impossible task outside a decolonizing methodology equipped to support subaltern researchers in shattering the colonizing neuromyths that are employed to sustain asymmetrical relations of power in the field and within society.

Disrupting the commonsense of modernity

In an alarming study about the allure of neuroscientific explanations and neuromyths, Weisberg et al. (2015) showed that people find explanations more satisfying when they contain irrelevant neuroscience information and then offer a number of reasons as to why this may be. The first reason offered is that explanations that reference the "hard" sciences are seen as generally more legitimate across disciplines, with an even more pronounced effect in psychology, which holds a general bias toward making psychological explanations sound "more scientific." A second explanation offered is that people are intuitively dualist. Yet another is that people tend to embrace causal or commonsensical explanations and are particularly biased toward teleological information that provides evidence of an ultimate cause for an event. And, finally, the authors assert that it is possible that neuroscience seduces because of a general epistemological preference within American society to gravitate toward reductive explanations.

However, what is missing from these arguments is an acknowledgment of the commonsensical manner in which Western scientific ideology conditions the unscientifically oriented masses to privilege science and, thus, to see with authority anything considered to be scientific. As such, human beings are socialized through their education to prefer reductionist, causal, dualist scientific conclusions, without concern for the knowledge and wisdom that is disallowed and erased in the process (Smith, 1999). Science has so successfully managed to limit rationality and garner authority over knowledge that we tend to simply acquiesce to this commonsensical socialization. The fact is, it is neither our brains nor biology that make us susceptible to science's exploitations. This ideological phenomenon occurs by epistemological design, not the nature of human beings.

As critics have asserted, "Both psychology and education in their institutional forms became absorbed by the 'modern', a project in which psychological science offered simultaneously both to individualize and to homogenize all human functioning as part of an underlying commitment to progress" (Billington, 2007, p. 869). Neuroscience then and brain-based education, in specific, like phrenology before it, are popular perhaps because of the underlying promise of modernization it offers through methodologies that produce tangible economic results. As the studies on the allure of neuroscience demonstrate, modernity has a "darker side" (Mignolo, 2011, p. 3), such that, in the popularization of neuroscience and its methodologies in everyday life and as part of "global modernities," we are once again forgetting the implications of "global colonialities" (p. 3) tied to the advancement of interests held by the wealthy and powerful.

Deconstructing economic interests

As Weisberg et al. (2015) and others have demonstrated, most people simply trust anything with a scientific explanation, name, or a picture of the brain attached (McCabe & Castel, 2008; Lindell & Kidd, 2013). In this way, the hegemony of empirical science contributes much to the accumulation of capital. The economic consequences of the global prevalence of neuromyths (Howard-Jones, 2014) have been well documented. The billion-dollar brain based educational industry aside, neuromyths from *Baby-Einstein* and *The Mozart Effect* to *The Myth of Three* (Howard-Jones, 2014) and programs packaged to cure learning disabilities (Goswami, 2006) lay the foundation of a political economy where bad science is shaping policy and misusing public funds in the name of so-called evidence-based education (Howard-Jones, 2014).

So, it is not just that notions of personhood are being radically transformed in this new and growing medicalized context (Vidal, 2009), where neuroscience pushes us toward a reality where "we are our brains" and no more than our "neurochemical selves" (Rose, 2003, 2007). Yet, what is taking place on a mass scale, particularly as we move toward an increasing discourse of the so-called Fourth Industrial Revolution, neuroscientific notions are being used dramatically to build neoliberal economic models of educational investment (Heckman, 2008) that homogenize students and reproduce growing economic inequality, despite the equity opportunity discourse. In this way, De Vos and Pluth (2015) contend that "the prefix neuro- has won its final battle" not just because "it has conquered critique itself" (p. 22), but because it has done so while turning a hefty profit among the few.

Conclusion

The purpose of my decolonizing interpretive study was to re-think and re-envision the field of MBE, looking specifically at the lack of engagement with social justice concerns in order to: (1) critique the dominant epistemology of science that reproduces inequalities, not just within the field itself but in its intended practice; and (2) move toward the formulation of a social justice paradigm of MBE that supports conditions for an emancipatory and humanizing view of teachers, students, and brain-based educational practices, through a decolonizing interpretive methodology (Darder, 2014). As one might recognize from the discussion here, this would have been an utterly impossible task utilizing traditional reductive methodologies, anchored in Eurocentric values of distanced objectivity and reductive reasoning. In direct contrast, this study first sought to challenge and dismantle discursively the deep hegemonic epistemologies and structures at work in the field. This disruption was a necessary first step toward opening up the field to re-inventing itself, using a decolonizing lens that can move us toward creating a new multidimensional, fluid, and emancipatory vision for the field, grounded in a liberatory ethical commitment to contend with the needs of the most disenfranchised.

Hence, one of the significant principles of a decolonizing interpretive methodology with respect to educational research is then to engage the dominant literature on pedagogy, curriculum, methodology, and schooling, with the aim of disrupting dominant epistemologies and building decolonizing forms of knowledge (Darder, 2015). In the case of MBE, the first step was to disrupt the primary stance shaped by a positivist epistemology, where research tends to become a means for the promotion of Western scientific thought and its political economic project of conquest. In fact, an argument of decolonizing interpretive methodology is that research needs to "unveil and destabilize existing structures of power that perpetuate the material and social oppression of the most vulnerable populations" (Darder, 2015, p. 4), rather than to contribute to the reproduction and perpetuation of these oppressive structures.

Once this important disruptive step has taken place, a new paradigm can begin to emerge, informed by decolonizing principles of knowledge deconstruction and reconstruction, as well as an ethical commitment to socially just educational practices. Rejecting the scientific gold standard of positivist research—whether quantitative or qualitative—as the objective and unbiased search for knowledge, a decolonizing research paradigm recognizes that all knowledge is ideological, political, cultural, historical, spiritual, and encourages a deep understanding and recognition of the interconnectedness and holism of nature, moving beyond boundaries of objective measurement (Smith, 1999).

Moreover, such a paradigm entails responsibility for maintaining harmonious relationships among people, nature, and all life, and placing ethics and context, not neutral notions of objectivity, at the center of all research. This paradigm follows then an itinerant, rhizomic, and fluid approach to knowledge production, honoring multiple ways of knowing along a horizontal field, encouraging dialogue and recognizing the interdependent nature of knowledge in the world. Such a decolonizing research methodology is organically interconnected (rather than discipline based) and embraces epistemological diversity, in ways that open opportunities for engagement across difference. Instead of valuing abstract knowledge derived from experiments and controlled variables, knowledge is derived through a decolonizing methodology that respects all processes of perceiving, thinking, acting, and coming to know that evolve through human experience, within the context of power relations in the larger society. It is, however, as I have sought to show here, impossible to envision decolonizing forms of knowledge, without the willingness to enter deeply into the work of disrupting and questioning the dominant knowledge that exists. Hence, we must first strive toward "emancipatory reformulation of the conceptual or ideological interrelationships that exist between theoretical explanations and practical applications" (Darder, 2014, p. 74), before we can begin to posit new ways of knowing within education that can support our efforts toward social change.

Notes

1 This chapter is based on my doctoral dissertation research entitled *A Critical Interrogation of the Mind, Brain, and Education Movement: Toward a Social Justice Paradigm.* The study can be retrieved from https://pqdtopen.proquest.com/doc/2115213913.html?FMT=ABS.
2 The reference here is to Darder's articulation of biculturalism, which engages with the tensions that exist for bicultural educators from subordinated cultural communities who must contend with dominant ideologies in their process of teaching, learning, and research. See Darder (2012) for a discussion of this critical understanding of biculturalism.

References

Alberts, B. (2010). Policy-making needs sciences. *Science* 330, 1287.

Apple, M. (1990). *Ideology and curriculum* (2nd edition). New York: Routledge.

Bao, Y., & Pöppel, E. (2012). Anthropological universals and cultural specifics: Conceptual and methodological challenges in cultural neuroscience. *Neuroscience & Biobehavioral Reviews* 36(9), 2143–2146. doi:10.1016/j.neubiorev.2012.06.008.

Bergeron, K. E. (2017). *Challenging the cult of self-esteem in education: Education, psychology, and the subaltern self.* New York: Routledge.

Billington, T. (2017). Educational inclusion and critical neuroscience: Friends or foes? *International Journal of Inclusive Education* 21(8), 866–880. doi:10.1080/13603116.2017.1283717.

Bowles, S., & Gintis, H. (2011). *Schooling in capitalist America: Educational reform and the contradictions of economic life.* Chicago: Haymarket Books.

Braidotti, R. (2013). *The posthuman.* Malden, MA: Polity Press.

Choudhury, S., & Slaby, J. (Eds.) (2011). *Critical neuroscience: A handbook of the social and cultural contexts of neuroscience.* West Sussex: Wiley-Blackwell.

Christoff, K. (2008). Applying neuroscientific findings to education: The good, the tough, and the hopeful. *Mind, Brain, and Education* 2(2), 55–58. doi:10.1111/j.1751-228X.2008.00031.x.

Connell, R. (2007). *Southern theory: The global dynamics of knowledge in social science.* Cambridge: Polity.

Connor, D. J., Gabel, S. L., Gallagher, D. J., & Morton, M. (2008). Disability studies and inclusive education—implications for theory, research, and practice. *International Journal of Inclusive Education* 12(5–6), 441–457. doi:10.1080/13603110802377482.

Cozolino, L. (2013). *The social neuroscience of education: Optimizing attachment and learning in the classroom.* New York: Norton.

Darder, A. (2012). *Culture and power in the classroom: Educational foundations for the schooling of bicultural students.* New York: Routledge.

Darder, A. (2014). *Freire and education.* New York: Routledge.

Darder, A. (2015). Decolonizing interpretive research: A critical bicultural methodology for social change. *International Education Journal: Comparative Perspectives* 14(2), 63–77.

Darder, A. (2017). *Reinventing Paulo Freire: A pedagogy of love.* New York: Routledge.

Darder, A. (2018). Decolonizing interpretive research: Subaltern sensibilities and the politics of voice. *Qualitative Research Journal* 18(2), 94–104. doi:10.1108/QRJ-D-17-00056.

Davies, P. (1999). What is evidence-based education? *British Journal of Educational Studies* 47(2), 108–121. doi:10.1111/1467-8527.00106.

De Freitas, E. (2012). The classroom as rhizome: New strategies for diagramming knotted interactions. *Qualitative Inquiry* 18(7), 557–570.

De Vos, J., & Pluth, E. (2015). *Neuroscience and critique: Exploring the limits of the neurological turn.* New York: Routledge.

Dudley-Marling, C., & Burns, M. B. (2014). Two perspectives on inclusion in the United States. *Global Education Review* 1(1), 14–31. Retrieved from http://ger.mercy.edu/index. php/ger/article/view/10.

Fischer, K. W. (2009). Mind, brain, and education: Building a scientific groundwork for learning and teaching. *Mind, Brain, and Education* 3(1), 3–16. doi:10.1111/j.1751-228X.2008.01048.x.

Fischer, K. W., & Daniel, D. B. (2009). Need for infrastructure to connect research with practice in education. *Mind, Brain, and Education* 3(1), 1–2. doi:10.1111/j.1751–1228X.2008.01054.x.

Fischer, K. W., Goswami, U., & Geake, J. (2010). The future of educational neuroscience. *Mind, Brain, and Education* 4(2), 68–80. doi:10.1111/j.1751-228X.2010.01086.x.

Fischer, K. W., Daniel, D. B., Immordino-Yang, M. H., Stern, E., Battro, A., & Koizumi, H. (2007). Why mind, brain, and education? Why now? *Mind, Brain, and Education* 1(1), 1–2. doi:10.1111/j.1751-228X.2007.00006.x.

Four Arrows, D., Cajete, G., & Lee, J. (2009). *Critical neurophilosophy and indigenous wisdom.* Boston: Sense Publishers.

Freire, P. (1985). *The politics of education: Culture, power, and liberation.* Westport: Bergin and Garvey.

Freire, P. (1998). *Pedagogy of freedom: Ethics, democracy, and civic courage.* Lanham: Rowman & Littlefield.

Freire, P. (2000). *Pedagogy of the oppressed.* New York: Continuum.

Freire, P., & Macedo, D. (1987). *Literacy: Reading the word and the world.* London: Routledge.

Fromm, E. (1976). *To have or to be?* New York: Harper & Row.

Giroux, H. A. (1981). *Ideology, culture and the process of schooling.* Philadelphia: Temple University Press.

Goswami, U. (2006). Neuroscience and education: From research to practice? *Nature Reviews Neuroscience*, AOP, published online April 12, 2006, 1–7. doi:10.1038/nrn1907.

Gould, S. J. (1996). *The mismeasure of man.* New York: W. W. Norton & Company.

Gramsci, A. (1971). *Selections from the prison notebooks.* New York: International Publishers.

Grosfoguel, R. (2011). Decolonizing post-colonial studies and paradigms of political-economy: Transmodernity, decolonial thinking, and global coloniality. *Transmodernity: Journal of Peripheral Cultural Production of the Luso-Hispanic World* 1(1). Retrieved from https:// cloudfront.escholarship.org/dist/prd/content/qt21k6t3fq/qt21k6t3fq.pdf.

Grotzer, T. A. (2011). Public understanding of cognitive neuroscience research findings: Trying to peer beyond enchanted glass. *Mind, Brain, and Education* 5(3), 108–114. doi:10.1111/j.1751–1228X.2011.01118.x.

Haraway, D. (1988). Situated knowledges: The science question in feminism and the privilege of partial perspective. *Feminist Studies* 14(3), 575–599. doi:10.2307/3178066.

Heckman, J. J. (2008). Schools, skills, and synapses. *Economic Inquiry* 46(3), 289–324.

Henry, J. (1963) *Culture against man.* New York: Random House.

hooks, b. (1994) *Teaching to transgress: Education as the practice of freedom.* New York: Routledge.

Howard-Jones, P. (2014). Neuroscience and education: Myths and messages. *Nature Reviews Neuroscience*, AOP, published online October 15, 2014, 1–8. doi:10.1038/nrn3817.

Illich, I. (1971). *Deschooling society.* New York: Harper & Row.

Jackson, P. W. (1968). *Life in classrooms.* New York: Holt, Rinehart, and Winston.

Janson, E. E., & Paraskeva, J. M. (2015). Curriculum counter-strokes and strokes: Swimming in non-existent epistemological rivers. *Policy Futures in Education* 13(8), 949–967.

Jencks, C. (1972). *Inequality: A reassessment of the effect of family and schooling in America.* New York: Basic.

Kincheloe, J. (1993). *Toward a critical politics of teacher thinking: Mapping the postmodern.* Granby, MA: Bergin and Garvey.

Kingsmith, A. T. (2017). On rupture: An intervention into epistemological disruptions of Machiavelli, Hobbes, and Hume. *The Journal of Speculative Philosophy* 31(4), 594–608.

Kirmayer, L. (2012). The future of critical neuroscience. In S. Choudhury & J. Slaby (Eds.), *Critical neuroscience: A handbook of the social and cultural contexts of neuroscience* (pp. 367–384). Chichester: Wiley-Blackwell.

Knox, R. (2016). Mind, brain, and education: A transdisciplinary field. *Mind, Brain, and Education* 10(1), 4–9. doi:10.1111/mbe.12102.

Kozol, J. (1967). *Death at an early age: The destruction of the hearts and minds of Negro children in the Boston public schools.* Boston: Houghton Mifflin.

Lindell, A. K., & Kidd, E. (2013). Consumers favor "right brain" training: The dangerous lure of neuromarketing. *Mind, Brain, and Education* 7(1), 35–39. doi:10.1111/mbe.12005.

Mate, G. (2000). *Scattered: How attention deficit disorder originates and what you can do about it.* New York: Plume.

Mate, G. (2011). *Scattered minds: A new look at the origins and healing of attention deficit disorder.* Toronto: Vintage Canada.

McCabe, D. P., & Castel, A. D. (2008). Seeing is believing: The effect of brain images on judgments of scientific reasoning. *Cognition* 107, 343–352.

Mignolo, W. (2007). Introduction: Coloniality of power and de-colonial thinking. *Cultural Studies* 21(2–3), 155–167. doi:10.1080/09502380601162498.

Mignolo, W. (2011). *The darker side of western modernity: Global futures, decolonial options.* Durham, NC: Duke University Press.

Newcombe, N. S. (2013). Educating to use evidence in thinking about education. *Mind, Brain, and Education* 7(2), 147–150. doi:10.1111/mbe.12018.

Nickerson, R. S. (1998). Confirmation bias: A ubiquitous phenomenon in many guises. *Review of General Psychology* 2(2), 175–220. Retrieved from https://pdfs.semanticscholar.org/70c9/3e5e38a8176590f69c0491fd63ab2a9e67c4.pdf

Paraskeva, J. (2011). *Conflicts in curriculum theory.* New York: Palgrave.

Paraskeva, J. (2016). *Curriculum epistemicide: Toward an itinerant curriculum theory.* New York: Routledge.

Pasquinelli, E. (2011). Knowledge and evidence-based education: Reasons, trends, and contents. *Mind, Brain, and Education* 5(4), 186–195.

Pasquinelli, E. (2012). Neuromyths: Why do they exist and persist? *Mind, Brain, and Education* 6(2), 89–96. doi:10.1111/j.1751-228X.2012.01141.x.

Quijano, A. (2000). Coloniality of power, eurocentrism, and Latin America. *Napantla: Views from the South* 1(3), 533–580.

Rizvi, F., Lingard, B., & Lavia, J. (2006). Postcolonialism and education: Negotiating a contested terrain. *Pedagogy, Culture and Society* 14(3), 249–262.

Rose, N. (2003). Neurochemical selves. *Society* 41(1), 46–59. doi:10.1007/BF02688204.

Rose, N. (2007). *The politics of life itself: Biomedicine, power, and subjectivity in the twenty- first century.* Princeton: Princeton University Press.

Rose, S. (2006). *The twenty first-century brain: Explaining, mending and manipulating the mind.* London: Vintage.

Samuels, B. M. (2009). Can the differences between education and neuroscience be overcome by mind, brain, and education? *Mind, Brain, and Education* 3(1), 45–55. doi:10.1111/j.1751-228X.2008.01052.x.

Santos, B. de Sousa (2005). *Democratizing democracy: Beyond the liberal democratic canon.* London: Verso.

Santos, B. de Sousa (Ed.) (2007a). *Another knowledge is possible: Beyond northern epistemologies.* New York: Verso.

Santos, B. de Sousa (Ed.) (2007b). *Cognitive justice in a global world: Prudent knowledges for a decent life.* Lanham: Lexington.

Santos, B. de Sousa (2007c). Beyond abyssal thinking: From global lines to ecologies of knowledges. *Review (Fernand Braudel Center)* 30(1), 45–89. Retrieved from www.jstor.org/stable/40241677.

Scott, J. A., & Curran, C. M. (2010). Brains in jars: The problem of language in neuroscientific research. *Mind, Brain, and Education* 4(3), 149–155. doi:10.1111/j.1751-228X.2010.01093.x.

Shiva, V. (1993). *Monocultures of the mind: Perspectives on biodiversity and biotechnology.* New York: Zed Books.

Smith, L. T. (1999). *Decolonizing methodologies.* London: Zed.

Smith, R. M., Gallagher, D., Owen, V. , & Skrtic, T. M. (2009). Disability studies in education. *In* J. Andrzejewski, M. P. Baltodano , & L. Symcox *(Eds.), Social justice, peace, and environmental education: Transformative standards (pp.* 235–251). New York: Routledge.

Spivak, G. C. (1988). *Can the subaltern speak?*Basingstoke: Macmillan.

Steiner, S. S., Krank, H. M., Bahruth, R. E., & McLaren, P. (2004). *Freireian pedagogy, praxis, and possibilities: Projects for the new millennium.* London: Routledge.

Strom, K. (2015). Teaching as assemblage: Negotiating learning and practice in the first year of teaching. *Journal of Teacher Education* 66(4), 321–333.

Szűcs, D., & Goswami, U. (2007). Educational neuroscience: Defining a new discipline for the study of mental representations. *Mind, Brain, and Education* 1(3), 114–127. doi:10.1111/j.1751-228X.2007.00012.x.

Tardif, E., Doudin, P. A., & Meylan, N., (2015). Neuromyths among teachers and students. *Mind, Brain, and Education* 9(1), 50–59. doi:10.1111/mbe.12070.

US Department of Education, Office of the Deputy Secretary. (2002). *U.S. Department of Education strategic plan for 2002–2007* (ED Document No. 466 025). Retrieved from www.ed.gov/pubs/stratplan2002-07/index.html.

Vidal, F. (2009). Brainhood, anthropological figure of modernity. *History of the Human Sciences* 22(1), 5–36. doi:10.1177/0952695108099133.

Weisberg, D. S., Taylor, J., & Hopkins, E. (2015). Deconstructing the seductive allure of neuroscience explanations. *Judgment and Decision Making* 10(5), 429–441. Retrieved from https://repository.upenn.edu/neuroethics_pubs/132.

Wexler, P. (1976). *The sociology of education: Beyond inequality.* Indianapolis: The Bobbs-Merrill Company.

6

EMANCIPATORY RE-READINGS[1]

Terrelle Billy Sales

> Stand fast therefore in the liberty wherewith Christ has made us free and be not
> entangled again with the yoke of bondage.
>
> *(Galatians 5:1)*

In examining the history of education in America, from its religious inception to its
secular manifestation, and the overall lack of clarity surrounding the missions of not
only secular institutions, but also Christian institutions of higher education, students
are left longing for a greater experience. The purpose of the university is based on
noble purposes, ideally to pursue truth, through the opening of minds to promoting
the idea of redefining the possible (Blauner, 1970). However, most of these institutions neither know nor care enough to engage in the histories or lived experiences of
the diverse populations they serve. Hence, I would argue that a nation that refuses to
define education more inclusively, as well as to grapple with its underlying purpose
to humanity is a nation that, as Carter G. Woodson (1990) declared in 1933, is
severely *mis-educated*. Similarly, defining the purpose of education, due to the
increased secularization and colonization of American subaltern populations, has
become a very difficult task. America continues to propagate the necessity of higher
education and generate billions of dollars a year off of this premise, yet continues to
fail to substantiate the claim by actively providing a meaningful and purposeful
educational experience for its constituents, particularly African American/Black and
indigenous populations.

A personal example is useful here. I identify as Black. I identify as Christian. This
is a conscious decision made in my attempt to develop an identity based off limited
knowledge, experience, and truth presented to me through a lens shaped by an
education and spiritual formation imbued in the colonial Eurocentric tradition. I
often wondered why my educational experience did not provide the fulfillment
promised by the "American Dream"—an idea still perpetuated at many campuses

throughout the country. The ideals, history, language, pedagogical strategies, education, and ideologies of my education were all filtered through a racializing lens that uplifted and favored the dominant culture, all while relegating the majority of subaltern populations to a state of social and material impoverishment. Consequently, as a Black Christian, these two aspects of my identity seem forever pitted against each other in an ethereal struggle to develop an empowered identity within a so-called postcolonial nation, which remains steeped in Eurocentric epistemological principles still predicated on an exclusionary vision of humanity.

Thinking back on my academic formation and as a Black male in the United States, I never felt that my educational experience provided me the opportunity to engage both cognitively and intellectually with my Black identity or my Christian faith. Hence, I was never afforded the value of critically analyzing what it meant to be a Black Christian in an academic setting. Entering my college years, I purposefully chose to attend private Christian institutions of higher education with the resolve of having this experience but, sadly, it never materialized. As a Black student at both the undergraduate and graduate levels, I was never afforded the opportunity to engage critically with my identity as it related to educational and spiritual formation. Absent from both the curriculum and pedagogical practices was a critical perspective of Christianity and its liberatory influence on the Black experience in America.

As a student in a teacher education program, I yearned to learn about the pedagogy of Jesus Christ the teacher, as examined through a decolonizing epistemological and ontological lens that engaged my history and the conditions of my social location within society. And although Christian values and morals were assumed to be the norm for all students at the schools in which I studied, I still found myself only able to engage in theological, ethnic, ethical, and Christocentric matters by way of personal conversations, books, articles, and in my participation at my local church. In my personal experience, matters of identity and knowledge formation for Black Christian students are essential to our personal, social, and intellectual development. Hence, separation of theology and education become problematic, for both these two conceptual orientations have contributed profoundly to the formation of Black identity in America (Dancy, 2010; Gaines, 2010; Jett, 2010; Mitchell, 2010; Reyes, 2010). Hence, I strongly argued that theology and education should be embraced and utilized in tandem to produce a more holistic educational experience for Black Christian students. This fundamental premise became then the catalyst for my decolonizing interpretive study, which sought to unveil an emancipatory pedagogy of Jesus Christ.

An abundance of research over the last century has borne witness to the fact that Eurocentric epistemologies have permeated the pedagogical practices and ideologies of the majority of educators. Navigating life as an African American male from an impoverished background has provided its fair share of challenges; however, to experience racialized epistemologies reproduced and reinforced in educational institutions from kindergarten through high school has also created a unique set of challenges for Black students. As a student, I rarely felt affirmed throughout my academic formation. The teaching styles, instructional techniques, and pedagogical practices all seemed to paint a picture of an academic student who was supposed to be me, yet differed greatly from what I felt was essential to life, learning, and being. When the image on the canvas was finished, the portrait thought to be me, in actuality looked eerily unfamiliar. The image was not steeped in my culture, my background, or my race; it was quite the opposite. It was as if I were being colonized and forced to assimilate into an academic society that only accepted certain ways of thinking, speaking, and doing. The final portrait resembled many other likenesses produced by the educational system, none of which differed significantly from the others.

The deep yearning for my educational experience to not only affirm my identity, but also to cultivate my intellectual curiosity and spiritual formation, continues to be the driving force behind my insatiable appetite to learn. The absence of this kind of education for marginalized, culturally, and intellectually oppressed populations has been the catalyst for educational reform in the United States. It is an injustice for the educational system to function as an institution for the social reproduction of oppressive curricula and pedagogical practices (Duncan-Andrade & Morrell, 2008). This sets the perfect conditions for emancipatory practices that demand us to re-engage with the elements that make up our epistemological understandings of knowledge and power constructs in education.

Moreover, as a Black Christian male living in America, to some observers, I am a walking contradiction. The very faith that I hold dear and to which I have devoted my life, could very well be seen as the same faith used to justify and sustain acts of oppression and injustice toward my ancestors. On the surface, the Black experience in a society heavily influenced by Western colonial thought is one of severe oppression; Christianity, then, has been steeped in dogma justifying the proliferation of institutionalized racism, classism, sexism, inequality, and many other forms of dehumanization. However, when the Scriptures are critically examined, a Gospel of love, acceptance, and compassion is uncovered, which has been the driving cultural force of the Black Church in America. From this perspective, we have created a decolonizing expression of the Gospel, which seeks to emancipate the oppressed—a Gospel that both transcends and encapsulates all colors, ethnicities, cultures, and socioeconomic status (Galatians 3:26–28). As such, we have enacted within the Black Church a Gospel that epistemologically sits outside the hegemonic religious influences of the West. Hence, it was through the subaltern sensibilities of this decolonizing perspective that I sought to discover emancipatory re-readings of the pedagogy of Christ, by way of a decolonizing interpretive methodology (Darder, 2015a, 2018).

Foundation for emancipatory re-reading

For the pendulum in education to swing toward a more liberating direction, teaching strategies, philosophies, and theory have to undergo a rigorous process of critique. Freire (1970), a founding proponent of critical pedagogy, proposed that education should serve as a humanizing force to end oppression. He argued that students should learn within conditions that empower them to critically reflect on their social and historical realities, within their respective communities, in order to adequately engage and counter oppression in all its forms. As such, students and teachers should constantly be engaging in a dialectically grounded manner in the interest of an evolving process of conscientization, which can critically engage with the social, political, and economic conflicts and contradictions that impact their lives daily. Henry Giroux (2010), as does Darder in her decolonizing interpretive methodology, builds upon Freire's (1970) *pedagogy of the oppressed* as a praxis-oriented practice, guided by passion and political commitment, to create the condition for subaltern communities to develop a consciousness of freedom with which they can critically engage and challenge authoritarian tendencies, connect knowledge to power, and develop the skills to take constructive social action. When this framework is implemented, it serves as an effective means for transforming individual and collective consciousness society.

Critical pedagogy is rooted in the struggle to emancipate students and teachers from oppressive systems that permeate the hegemonic paradigm of education (Freire, 1970, 1998a). Critical pedagogues concur that this method of educational theory and practice provides educators and researchers with more accurate and culturally sensitive methods in understanding the roles all institutions of learning play in shaping and reshaping society (Duncan-Andrade & Morrell, 2008; Darder et al., 2003; Darder, 2012; hooks, 1994; Freire, 1970). One of the major charges of critical pedagogy is to "disclose and challenge the reproductive role schools play in political and cultural life" (Duncan-Andrade & Morrell, 2008, p. 2). As Darder (2012, 2015b) has repeatedly shown in her work, it is impossible to build on the tenets of critical pedagogy without first properly comprehending the principles upon which it is built. Within critical theory is a dialectical relationship that persistently intertwines the individual and society (Wardekker & Miedema, 1997). Emerging from critical thinkers countering capitalism and its reproduction of social, political, and educational systems of oppression, the critical principles that inform a decolonizing interpretive methodology are firmly established not solely as a method of knowledge production, but as a way of thinking, *being*, knowing, and understanding the world (Darder, 2012, 2015b; Darder et al., 2009; Giroux, 1983; Gutek, 2004; Kirylo, 2011).

The studies of decolonizing interpretive researchers are then informed by principles rooted and formulated in critical theory. From this perspective, education is obstinately concerned with answering one question: What is the purpose of education within an oppressive society? The optimal concern of the critical subaltern researcher peering through the lens of critical theory is the sociopolitical forces that continue to shape and reshape injustice and inequality (Darder et al., 2009). There must be then an intentional and consistent pursuit to engage the individual and society in a consistent dialogue rooted in emancipatory principles infused with democracy and freedom (McLaren, 1989). Critical thought is considered essential then to building meaningful connections among and across members of society, in order to properly influence society and challenge harmful epistemological constructions and misreading that continue to oppress subaltern populations (Gramsci, 1971).

Moreover, the ultimate aim of decolonizing interpretive research is to oppose and critique the hegemonic social paradigms predicated on capitalism, which seek to both normalize and quantify the human experience in an effort to control it. According to Foley et al. (2015), "what traditional theory lacks is a clear connection to the subjectivity of individuals and society, and is predicated on the notion of positivism in the sciences" (p. 133). Critical theoretical forms of knowledge construction, in contrast, focus consistently on creating the necessary conditions for more profound questioning of the values and structures that sustain gross inequalities in the world. Questioning society; questioning democracy; questioning self within society and democracy; questioning of education; questioning of politics; questioning of religion; questioning of the individual; questioning of the individual within education, politics, and religion—these are considered essential questions to a decolonizing interpretive study, which must be consistently engaged, if social transformation is our aim. In short, decolonizing interpretive research "questions the value-laden curriculum of everyday life … the power structures that manipulate rationality and truth … and how subjectivity becomes a political ontology" (Foley et al., 2015, pp. 113–114).

This critical theoretical foundation is not meant to remain an abstract exercise, but rather it is meant to support new ways of thinking that provide decolonizing researchers, educators, theorists, psychologists, and others a framework from which to both react and respond to hegemonic epistemologies, but also to address problems head on, through developing a critical praxis (Breunig, 2005; Gibbs, 1997), predicated upon what Darder (2018) terms subaltern sensibilities. The critical foundation that informs a decolonizing interpretive framework seeks to move society toward a praxis of knowledge production that embraces the beauty of human differences, yet also recognizes differences also require emancipatory critique, specifically with respect to the consequences of hegemonic conditions on the lives of those who have been historically marginalized and oppressed.

With this, hope, justice, love, and compassion are synonymous with the values of decolonizing subaltern researchers, where our efforts to name and know that world is anchored in our pursuit of liberation. There is a visceral interconnectedness or sensibility shaped by these elements that motivates the decolonizing subaltern researcher to seek new understanding of phenomenon that can support critical approaches and strategies for liberatory possibilities in the world. This approach functions, then, as a decolonizing framework that consistently informs the emancipatory re-reading of social phenomenon and, by so doing, generates transformative social action based on the analysis subaltern researchers bring to their labor.

Decolonizing knowledge

Education is an essential dimension of democratic life and significant to the development of conscientious citizens who are committed to culturally democratic outcomes (Darder, 2012). Despite democratic rhetoric in the arena of methodology, the hegemonic culture of research has traditionally been marred with oppressive curricula, fraught of "ideologies shaped by power, history, politics, culture and economics that do not align with and/or support the empowerment of culturally marginalized and economically disenfranchised students" (Darder et al., 2003, p. 11). Engaging the role of asymmetrical power relations and its oppressive impact on the lives of the disenfranchised, Gramsci (1971) proffered a deeper understanding of this system of social control and power through what he deems *cultural hegemony*.

According to Gramsci, in the process of traditional knowledge construction, hegemonic forces serve the interest of the dominant class and utilize power as a form of oppression, wielded in demonstrative efforts to actively silence subjugated populations (Giroux, 1985). In contrast, a decolonizing interpretive methodology "incorporates this notion of hegemony in order to demystify the asymmetrical power relations and social arrangements that sustain the interests of the ruling class" (Darder et al., 2003, p. 13). This ongoing process of critique here assists in the development of knowledge forms able to identify and challenge oppressive policies and practices, as well as support social action within the context of education and the larger society.

Just as emancipatory theory develops from the "hermeneutic demands of class-room praxis" (Gordon, 1986, p. 62), so too a decolonizing interpretive methodology emerges dialectically from the larger demands generated by the needs of subaltern populations (Darder, 2018). It is within this crucible of conflict and care, creativity and commitment that emancipatory research practices thrive, as subaltern researchers view our efforts, as Freire (1998a) would say, through a sense of *unfinishedness* and ourselves as lifelong learners, fully integrated as participants in the process of knowledge construction (Gordon, 1986). What provides credence to this decolonizing approach to research is not the mere words or philosophy, but the power of action that emerges from our critical reflection anchored in our lived experiences as sub-altern subjects of history (Freire, 1970). Similarly, subaltern researchers see the potential of decolonizing knowledge to serve as a catalyst for the evolution of critical consciousness, social change, and our collective capacity to redefine life in schools and beyond.

Freire (1998b) posits that teaching must function as an act of liberation. Along the same lines, Darder (2015a, 2018), as did Linda Tuhiwai Smith (1999) before her, asserts an understanding of decolonizing knowledge as a political act and, thus, with the revolutionary potential for generating decolonizing possibilities. However, in order to effectively unveil and challenge systems of oppression, decolonizing interpretive researchers must deconstruct questions of power, particularly with respect to how epistemological forms of violence are implicated in the oppression of indigenous and other subaltern populations. Hence, similar to the manner in which critical educators utilize the classroom as a vehicle for social transformation by creating the conditions for students to think critically about politics and society in their own lives and the world, so too decolonizing interpretive researchers seek to create a space with our studies to reflect a praxis of change. Power structures that are set up to persistently oppress marginalized and poverty-stricken communities must be radically reoriented to initiate the possibility for decolonizing structures that will, in the process, allow us to participate in the *reinventing of power* and, thus, provides us a space from which to launch emancipatory re-readings of oppressive conditions that have shaped our histories and the contemporary moment (Darder, 2002; Freire, 1998a).

Decolonizing interpretive research and the new visions that emerge are then concerned with liberating knowledge from traditional Eurocentric epistemologies that have served as a means for social reproduction complicit in perpetuating hegemonic ideologies of our times (Shor, 1992). Hence, to challenge normalized structures of traditional research paradigms, decolonizing research seeks to critically reflect on the characteristics and consequences of asymmetrical relations of power, in order to discover the emancipatory possibilities that exist beyond the *limit-situations* (Freire, 1970) that perpetuate and enact structures of oppression. It is also noteworthy that the emancipatory re-readings that emerge from this decolonizing research process are anchored in "relationships of self-determination, [which] serve as the impetus for this reflection on the need for a decolonizing community practice—one that cultivates political grace among those who aspire to create both social and material change" (Darder & Yiamouyiannis, 2009, p. 10).

Through engagement with the principle of emancipatory re-readings, my critical analysis of the Scriptures led to uncovering a critical pedagogy of Jesus Christ, which assisted me in illustrating the necessity for educational leaders to engage with the emancipatory possibilities inherent in the relationship between theology and education. By engaging in a critical theological and pedagogical analysis of the biblical Scriptures that speak to the life of Jesus Christ and his praxis—an emancipatory re-reading made possible by utilizing a decolonizing interpretive methodology—what emerged from my study was much more than simply another Westernized account of the human experience in relation to God and man. Through the process of emancipatory re-reading, a critical deconstruction of epistemicides (Paraskeva, 2011; Santos, 2005) embedded within the educational and theological constructs was carried out, which culminated in a liberatory vision of the pedagogy of Christ (Sales, 2017).

Re-reading the pedagogy of Christ

Dualism in the Western tradition makes the claim that mind and matter are two ontologically separate categories that extend to the epistemological domain (Bojabotseha, 2011). The epistemological dualism of Western Christianity then has functioned not only to perpetuate the othering of humanity, but also to separate human beings from nature and, thus, God from humanity. This is an epistemological problem related to how we make meaning and how we are conditioned to read the relationship between humanity and the Divine (Santos, 2015). Within this Westernized understanding of Christianity, often the focus of Christ is on how values are interpreted by others in terms of Christ's work. Yet, seldom is there critical engagement with Christ's words and actions as teacher.

By critically examining Jesus Christ as teacher, the aim of my study was to extend our understanding toward a more precise liberating Christ-centered praxis that could inform both Christian education and other disciplines in education from a critical emancipatory Christocentric lens. The goal to formulate a critical Christocentric framework useful to informing educational pedagogy, theory, theology, and leadership practices was developed. Through re-reading the Scriptures by way of a decolonizing interpretive research lens, I proffer a sustainable possibility in bridging the gap between theology and education, primarily by critically examining the praxis of Jesus Christ and His historical contributions toward challenging the oppression of racialized and marginalized communities in the Americas and around the world.

There are three central themes in relation to my study that best tie to the underlying emancipatory purpose of this decolonizing interpretive analysis. The first concerns itself with critical analysis as a human encounter, or "human moment" (De Lissovoy, 2010). Within human moments or encounters, humans engage in a dialectic focused on the transformative liberation of humanity and the world. This dialogue within and across the bodies of literature that informed my study is ongoing, steeped in hope and faith in subaltern researchers to possess the capacity to problematize their existential situations, through engaging in a decolonizing praxis (Berthoff, 1990; Freire, 1970; Gibbs, 1997).

The second theme aligns itself with the first but yields its essence in the understanding of conscientization (Freire, 1970). This outcome is directly linked to the process of critical reflection and dialogue within both critical pedagogy and liberation theology (Kirylo & Cone, 2011; Oldenski, 2002), which Darder (2015a, 2018) infuses in her articulation of a decolonizing interpretive methodology. Critical engagement is essential to liberatory pedagogical and research practices (Smith, 1999), in that it supports a transformative problem-posing approach, equipped to critically examine the conditions of students' lives in relation to the larger society.

The final and most important theme, which encapsulates the others, is the principle of love (Darder, 2002, 2011, 2017; Freire, 1973, 1995, 1998b; Oldenski, 2002). Teaching and research for the subaltern educator is understood fundamentally as "an act of love" (Darder, 1998), rooted in the ontological understanding that humans, as subjects of history, are social agents of change. Just as these themes are central to critical pedagogical practices, so too are they fundamental to a decolonizing interpretive methodology. Moreover, as should not be surprising, these themes also emerged in my emancipatory re-reading of a pedagogy of Jesus Christ—recognized, according to the liberation theologist Leonardo Boff (1978), as He who first introduced the world to a fuller understanding of the human being and God, through forms of critical emancipatory practice.

My emancipatory re-reading of the scriptures revealed the labor of Jesus Christ as *an act of love*; a love not merely built on emotion and feelings, but a love devoted to truth, conviction, and a commitment to dialectical relationship between humanity and God (Mark 10:17–22). Relative to His world and contexts mirroring the social, political, economic, educational, and spiritual conditions of His time, Jesus also calls for His learners to engage and develop social consciousness (John

4:1–26), informed by an ethics of liberation (Dussel, 2013)—where there is an uncompromising commitment to exist and labor in communion with the most vulnerable. Within the teachings of Christ, we also see unique human moments shared at a level of intensity unparalleled in scope and impact, that unfolded through the means of dialogue (John 21:15–17). The defining factor of Jesus's pedagogy, the element that sets His teaching apart from all others is, in fact, the component of unconditional love—a radical love expressed both in His life and praxis, through forgiveness and restoration (Sales, 2017). Conscientization, dialogue, human encounter, and teaching as an act of love—all indispensable qualities of critical educators posited by Freire (1998b)—are unmistakably present and enacted in the pedagogy of Jesus Christ. Through implementing a decolonizing interpretive approach, my study illustrated these elements and offered implications not only for subaltern researchers and critical educators, but also for educational leaders at the forefront of social justice work.

Conclusion

The articulation of a critical pedagogy of Christ that emerged from my study provides critical educators and researchers with a framework to identify liberatory principles of practice that deconstruct oppressive relationships and conditions that reinscribe the coloniality of power within both educational and theological contexts. It encompasses a pedagogy deeply informed by a Black cultural context and a decolonizing analysis that seeks to validate, liberate, and uplift us from humanity's suffering. Jesus in His critical praxis of love provides educators an example of liberatory ways of knowing and teaching that support a more just world, by way of dismantling colonizing forms of theological and educational practices and building, instead, organic and humanizing ways of encountering the world.

Utilizing a decolonizing interpretive methodology created a space for me, as a subaltern Christian researcher and educator, to partake in a comprehensive emancipatory re-reading of three major texts from the New Testament (John 4:1–26, Mark 10:17–22, John 21:15–17). The nature of this work necessitated a process by which critical inquiry provided a place to deconstruct traditional Western epistemologies surrounding theology and education. Decolonizing interpretive analysis serves then to provide subaltern researchers the counterhegemonic and decolonizing spaces to engage and critique dominant bodies of literature, while seeking serious and meaningful re-readings of our world (Darder, 2015a, 2018). This political and pedagogical labor of love constitutes an intrinsic call to challenge and disrupt one-dimensional Eurocentric epistemicides that have historically misappropriated and colonized our knowledge of Jesus Christ.

However, the urgency of liberation from oppressive dehumanizing social and material conditions often engenders in decolonizing researchers the resolve and fortitude to continue our journey toward restorative practices, rooted in love. What is to be learned from Jesus in His *human encounter* with the Rich Young Ruler in Mark 10:17–22? The ontological lesson first seeks to reconcile humanity to God and refocus our efforts toward greater service to each other. The episte-mological lesson here reconciles the divine relationship between love and truth and illuminates our finite capacity to see and experience truth outside of context and our human encounters. As subaltern educators, researchers, and educational leaders for social justice, we must critically commit ourselves to a decolonizing future, where our pedagogical, spiritual, and political relationships in the world are shaped by an undivided sense of solidarity and love for the well-being of all people.

Note

1   This chapter is based on my doctoral dissertation research entitled *An Emancipatory Pedagogy of Jesus Christ: Toward a Decolonizing Epistemology of Education and Theology*. The study can be retrieved from https://pqdtopen.proquest.com/doc/1957425543.html?FMT=ABS.

References

Berthoff, A. (1990). Paulo Freire's liberation pedagogy. *Language Arts* 67(4), 362–369. Retrieved from www.jstor.org/stable/41961745.

Blauner, R. (1970). The furious passage of the black graduate student: A comment. *Berkeley Journal of Sociology* 15, 212–214. Retrieved from www.jstor.org/stable/41035175.

Boff, L. (1978). *Jesus Christ liberator: A critical Christology for our time*. Maryknoll: Orbis Books.

Bojabotseha, T. P. (2011). Dualism and the social formation of South Africa. *African Journal of Hospitality, Tourism & Leisure* 1(3). Retrieved from www.academia.edu/4623175/Dua lism_and_the_Social_Formation_of_South_Africa.

Breunig, M. (2005). Turning experiential education and critical pedagogy theory into praxis. *Journal of Experiential Education* 28(2), 106–122.

Dancy, T. E. (2010). Faith in the unseen: The intersection(s) of spirituality and identity among African American males in college. *The Journal of Negro Education* 79(3), 416–432.

Darder, A. (1998). Teaching as an act of love: Reflections on Paulo Freire's contribution to our lives and our work. Occasional Paper Series. Los Angeles: California Association of Bilingual Education.

Darder, A. (2002). *Reinventing Paulo Freire: A pedagogy of love*. Boulder: Westview Press.

Darder, A. (2011). Unfettered bodies: Forging an emancipatory pedagogy of the flesh. *Counterpoints* 418, 343–359.

Darder, A. (2012). *Cultural and power in the classroom* (2nd edition). Boulder: Paradigm.

Darder, A. (2015a). Decolonizing interpretive research: A critical bicultural methodology for social change. *The International Educational Journal: Comparative Perspectives* 14(2), 63–77.

Darder, A. (2015b). *Freire and education*. New York: Routledge.

Darder, A. (2017). *Reinventing Paulo Freire: A pedagogy of love* (2nd edition). New York: Routledge.

Darder, A. (2018). Decolonizing interpretive research: Subaltern sensibilities and the politics of voice. *Qualitative Research Journal* 18(2), 94–104. https://doi.org/10.1108/QRJ-D-17-00056.

Darder, A., & Yiamouyiannis, Z. (2009). Cultivating political grace: Toward a decolonizing approach to community practice. In J. Lavia & M. Moore (Eds.), *Cross-cultural perspectives on policy and practice: Decolonizing community contexts* (pp. 10–27). London: Routledge.

Darder, A., Baltodano, M., & Torres, R. D. (2003). *The critical pedagogy reader*. London: Routledge.

Darder, A., Baltodano, M., & Torres, R. D. (2009). *The critical pedagogy reader*. New York: Routledge.

De Lissovoy, N. (2010). Rethinking education and emancipation: Being, teaching, and power. *Harvard Educational Review* 80(2), 203–221.

Duncan-Andrade, J., & Morrell, E. (2008). Contemporary developers of critical pedagogy. *Counterpoints* 285, 23–48.

Dussel, E. (2013). *Ethics of liberation: In the age of globalization and exclusion*. Durham, NC: Duke University Press.

Foley, J. A., Morris, D., Gounari, P., & Agostinone-Wilson, F. (2015). Critical education, critical pedagogies, Marxist education in the United States. *Journal for Critical Education Policy Studies* 13(3), 110–144.

Freire, P. (1970). *Pedagogy of the oppressed*. New York: Herder and Herder.

Freire, P. (1973). *Education as the practice of freedom: Education for critical consciousness*. Translated by M. B. Ramos. New York: Continuum.

Freire, P. (1995). The progressive teacher. In M. de Figuereido-Cowen & D. Gastaldo (Eds.), *Paulo Freire at the institute* (pp. 17–24). London: Institute of Education.

Freire, P. (1998a). *Pedagogy of freedom: Ethics, democracy, and civic courage*. Lanham: Rowman & Littlefield.

Freire, P. (1998b). *Teachers as cultural workers: Letters to those who are teach*. Boulder: Westview Press.

Gaines, R. W. (2010). Looking back, moving forward: How the civil rights era church can guide the modern black church in improving black student achievement. *The Journal of Negro Education* 79(3), 366–379.

Gibbs, E. (1997). Critical theory in critical education. *Ashland Theological Journal* 29, 57–65.

Giroux, H. A. (1983). *Theory and resistance in education: A pedagogy for the opposition*. South Hadley: Bergin & Garvey.

Giroux, H. A. (1985). Introduction. In P. Freire, *The politics of education: Culture power and liberation* (pp. xi–xxv). South Hadley: Bergin & Harvey Publishers.

Giroux, H. A. (2010). Lessons from Paulo Freire. *Chronicles of Higher Education* 57(9), 15–16.

Gordon, B. (1986). The use of emancipatory pedagogy in teacher education. *The Journal of Educational Thought (JET) / Revue De La Pensée Éducative* 20(2), 59–66. Retrieved from www.jstor.org/stable/23768744.

Gramsci, A. (1971). *Selections from the prison notebooks*. Translated by Q. Hoare & G. N. Smith. New York: International.

Gutek, G. L. (2004). *Philosophical and ideological voices in education*. Boston: Pearson Education.

hooks, b. (1994). *Teaching to transgress*. New York: Routledge.

Jett, C. C. (2010). "Many are called, but few are chosen": The role of spirituality and religion in the educational outcomes of "chosen" African American male mathematics majors. *The Journal of Negro Education* 79(3), 324–334. Retrieved from www.jstor.org/stable/20798352.

Kirylo, J. (2011). An overview of critical pedagogy: A case in point of Freirean inspired teaching. *Counterpoints* 385, 213–233. Retrieved from www.jstor.org/stable/42980931.

Kirylo, J., & Cone, J. (2011). Paulo Freire, Black theology of liberation, and liberation theology: A conversation with James H. Cone. *Counterpoints* 385, 195–212. Retrieved from www.jstor.org/stable/42980930.

McLaren, P. (1989). A pedagogy of possibility: Reflecting upon Paulo Freire's politics of education. *Educational Researcher* 28(2), 49–56.

Mitchell, R. W. (2010). Commentary: The African American church, education and self determination. *The Journal of Negro Education* 79(3), 202–204. Retrieved from www.jstor.org/stable/20798342.

Oldenski, T. (2002). The critical discourses of liberation theology and critical pedagogy. *Counterpoints* 38, 133–162. Retrieved from www.jstor.org/stable/42976928.

Paraskeva, J. (2011). *Conflicts in curriculum theory.* New York: Palgrave.

Reyes, J. (2010). Religiosity, religious schools, and their relationship with the achievement gap: A research synthesis and meta-analysis. *The Journal of Negro Education* 79(3), 263–279.

Sales, T. B. (2017). *An emancipatory pedagogy of Jesus Christ: Towards a decolonizing epistemology of education and theology* (Doctoral dissertation). Retrieved from https://pqdtopen.proquest.com/doc/1957425543.html?FMT=ABS (Publication Number 10622261).

Santos, B. de Sousa (2005). *Democratizing democracy: Beyond the liberal democratic canon.* London: Verso.

Santos, B. de Sousa (2015). *If God were a human rights activist.* Stanford: Stanford University Press.

Shor, I. (1992). *Empowering education: Critical teaching for social change.* Chicago: University of Chicago Press.

Smith, L. T. (1999). *Decolonizing methodologies.* New York: Zed Books.

Venn, C. (2000). *Occidentalism: Modernity and subjectivity.* London: Sage.

Wardekker, W., & Miedema, S. (1997). Critical pedagogy: An evaluation and a direction for reformulation. *Curriculum Inquiry* 27(1), 45–61. Retrieved from www.jstor.org/stable/1180054.

Woodson, C. G. (1990). *The mis-education of the Negro.* Trenton: Africa World Press.

AFTERWORD

Justice against epistemicides: decolonizing interpretive research as reiteration of itinerant praxis

João Paraskeva

> I even decided to become a practical man and intended to enter the railway office at the beginning of next year. Luckily – or perhaps I should say unluckily? – I did not get my post because of my bad hand-writing.
>
> *(Karl Marx, letter to Kugelman, December 28, 1862)*

Marx died in 1883, fifty years before Adolf Hitler was appointed German Chancellor in 1933. It would not take long for Hitler to implement his plans, explicitly written in his eugenic oeuvre *Mein Kampf*. In a huge popular rally held soon after he was sworn in, he screamed hysterically to the delusional, amorphous crowd, claiming, "I am founding a new era of truth" (Galeano, 2013, p. 32), a eugenic "Olympic leap in which those afflicted with the habit of thinking too much" (Galeano, 2013, p. 32) needed to be put to death. This "catapult," although framing one of the most horrendous moments in the recent history of Western Eurocentric Modernity, felicitously and frighteningly grasps our current era as well. We have arrived at the end of the second decade of the twenty first century fustigated and smashed by viral far-right fascism (Paraskeva, 2018), whose political roots are not detached from centuries of epistemological fascism and cognitive and cultural cleansing—propelled by the yoke of Western Eurocentrism—sustained by a humanity that needs a sub-humanity to exist (Santos, 2014) and a concomitant political economy that constructs a pastoral of the inevitability of oppression, exploitation, sub-humanity, and precarious labor hijacking workers' self-sufficiency, imposing a lethal nexus "modes of production – wages" (Perelman, 2000).

Such return to fascism, defined by Umberto Eco (2017) as Ur-fascism, is becoming viral and dangerous in its social constructions of reality and truth. Accordingly, these become fetishized and reified processes in which "data," "positivist truth," "empirical evidence," and "scientific literacy," based on Eurocentric epistemic parameters, become paradoxically the *oligarchy of the spectacle* (Hedges, 2009). The difference between a "wannabe Ur-fascist dictator" who claims that he can kill a person in cold blood or despicably attack indigenous and subaltern communities, and a real dictator that openly butchers—or gases—millions of his or her own people is just what Gaston Bachelard (2014) calls "poetics of space."

The constant violent attacks on green policies and global warming, public education, free health care, teachers and unions, bilingualism, biculturalism, specific immigrant communities, have been produced by belittling completely data and "empirical facts" and, in so doing, creating another truth momentum, the post-truth, a mythomaniac commonsensical canon that upgraded the Eurocentric myth propelling a new "reasoning." Dangerously, the populist Ur-fascist explosion we are facing currently cannot be reductively defined in terms of left, right, or center; it is a tsunami logic that floods the left, the center, and the right banks, a logic that starts its activity the very moment the incapability of liberal democracies to address crucial social issues became unquestionable. Such viral tsunami is "not an ideology, but a political logic – a way of thinking about politics" (Judis, 2016, p. 14; see also Kazin, 2017). Appallingly, Enlightenment-Modernity thereby regresses "to the mythology it has never been able to escape" (Horkheimer & Adorno, 2002, p. 20). Under the auspices of an unraveled global neoliberalism, our contemporary societies not only became defenceless and exposed, but they actually embrace a kind of discourse and praxis that was thought to be buried and resolved long ago: "populism with explicit fascist impulses" (Gil, 2018, p. 453).

Before such pandemonium, society eugenically moves forward, walking on a pavement of lies and false "non-existences" (Santos, 2005) that can only be accepted through the mechanisms of a ruthless system that through processes of reification disconnects the processes of social consciousness of the subject from certain phenomena by re-orienting it in other directions, which are more aligned with the maintenance of a given eugenic order, an order that, para-doxically, never tires of asserting itself more and more as such. Within such daily-routinized reification of social consciousness working class categories, minorities, indigenous and subaltern communities, woman and people of color become numbed, disposable, a recycled cargo, and surgically de-linked from their own mundane issues and racially blamed for lack of "cultural battery" and poor effort skills to fit within "the matrix."

While the commonsensical idea that indigenous and subaltern communities and individuals, immigrants, minorities, women, and people of color are genetically determined to submerge into terrifying lethal chaotic forms of existence is the supreme cult of the normalization of eugenic forms of cultural politics that became epitomized under far right leaders with fascist impulses, such as Donald Trump, Jair Bolsonaro, and others it is also impossible not to be incredulous to see specific fringes within such communities—what I have called elsewhere the sepoys of coloniality (Paraskeva, 2018) affected by such eugenic normalization—supporting such racialized forms of cultural politics that animalizes, bestializes, and sub-huma-nizes their own existence, a supreme example of a lethargic, reified rationale of social consciousness (Paraskeva, 2018).

Today, we are fighting a great battle—probably the greatest one—at the level of common sense, not necessarily between what is true and false and who holds the truth or not, which are such dichotomist constructions persistently exist in the socio-historical contexts; rather, the battle today is over the need to immediately torpedo the danger of a triumphant authoritarian populist far right fascist common sense that imposes the existence of "post-truth" as natural, as the real, as the newer reason, "a new era of truth." The post-truth is the non-existent existence that exists. Unfortunately, education and curriculum are not innocent in such "fact-cide." Submerged in a horrendous anti-intellectual intellectualism (Quantz, 2011), education, curriculum, and pedagogy is at the very core of this new eugenic metamorphosis of coloniality. Such post-truth momentum is indeed the new epistemological color of the colonial zone. The post-truth momentum unleashed a specific understanding of truth based on "because I say so" and "I can say so" rationale vs. science—conveniently instrumental and pragmatic—and its concomitant facts that are ostracized, trashed, and undermined (McIntyre, 2018).

The current approaches of leaders with despotic impulses, such as Donald Trump, Recep Tayyip Erdoğan, Kim Jong-un, Robert Mugabe, Narendra Modi, Viktor Mihály Orbán, Andrzej Duda, and Jair Bolsonaro, among others—with justifiable differences—have showed unequivocally that none of them based their policies on data or scientific readings and finds of the real(ity), but on the cult of body, image, panic, bestialization of the other, terror, spectacle, and a ferocious and merciless attack at a minimum rustle of dissent—even if moderate. Under the neoliberal deluge (Johnson, 2011), dissent, difference, conflict, discord, pluri-dimensionality are viewed as lethal threats that need to be terminated at any cost (Giroux, 2018). The way dominant and specific counter-dominant Western Eurocentric Modernity traditions and movements address the current shocking examples of this particular Ur-fascist post-truth oligarchy—such as Brexit (and its ambivalences), the inorganic yellow vest riots in France, and the Caravan from Honduras towards the United States—speaks volumes about an overtly arrogant cultural politics of denial (Abu-Lughod, 1989), a eugenic refusal to admit that the Western Cartesian Modernity model, in its hegemonic and counter-hegemonic matrixes with its arrogant claim to address global social issues, is not just moribund, it is dead.

The exclusion and impoverishment of African, Asian, and Latin American and other subaltern populations and their "indomitable will to survive" pushed modernity to an unsustainable point (Dussel, 2013). Modernity got lost irremediably between the real(ity) and representations of the real(ity). Modernity's final sentence was determined partially by modernity itself and its truly totalitarian cult, a cultural and economic napalm that attempted to erase all other epistemological manifestations, which paradoxically ended up being systematically reinforced and strengthened from the belligerent clashes with modernity. If colonialism is a crime against humanity, and colonialism and imperialism had no existence outside of modernity, then modernity is also not innocent in such crime against humanity. Not because it was inconsequential in dodging genocidal policies and practices, but precisely because its very existence relies on its capacity to perpetuate massive genocide.

Great achievements in areas such as space conquest and technologies have been reduced to a pale inconsequentiality for the massive majority of the world's population in the face of slavery, genocide, holocaust, poverty, inequality, social and cognitive apartheid, intergenerational injustice, and the temerity to change nature, among other issues. Painfully all of these sagas are at the very root of such modern societal tech advancements. History is not absolving, and it will not absolve, the Western Cartesian Modernity model. Modern Western Eurocentric reasoning was indeed a "misleading dream" (Harding, 2008, p. 23), which requires a commitment "to think alternatively about alternatives" (Santos, 2014) way above and beyond the Modern Western Eurocentric epistemological binaries of quantitative and or qualitative—an overt matrix of cognitive cleansing, and a superior weapon of de-humanization—embracing an emancipatory commitment which implies a de-territorialized approach and a critical itinerant position.

Decolonizing Interpretive Research is a clear and unequivocal voice against this dangerous post-truth moment, a primordial enzyme of the resurgence of fascism; it is much more than a cry of revolt—even though it express such state as well—at the swamp provoked by the dominant and counter-dominant movements; it is a sharp and fatal arrow at the very core of hermeneutics itself, drawn and accepted only, and only as possible and legitimate within the cognitive parameters imposed by the dictatorship of the Eurocentric consulate, where, on one hand, hegemonic movements impose a unique vision of the world and of being human, and, on the other, the counter-hegemonic movements impose a simplistic erroneous single vision of social transformation and emancipation, thus promoting segregated constructions of "reality," "truth," "beliefs," and "science"; in demythologizing hegemonic beliefs, Antonia Darder and colleagues insightfully challenge counter-hegemonic taboos as well, as the visibility of the former that has been constructed based on the invisibility of the latter (Chapter 4, this volume). The book bursts with this convenient marasmus in which epistemicide is perpetuated and declares that another hermeneutic is not only possible, but it is reality—a reality that fertilizes anti-colonial and de-colonial commitments triggered way back circa 1500s, right at the first encounter with white colonialism.

In this context, *Decolonizing Interpretive Research* is not just a vivid example of how modernity is (and always was) under the gun due the impossibility of perpetual submission from "the other" (Paraskeva, 2016, 2018), and that "the European game is definitely finished, and that it is necessary to find something else" (Fanon, 1963); it demonstrates a rich and robust web of indigenous and subaltern cognitive patterns that defy irremediably—without falling into the demagoguery cult of being a recipe—what Boaventura de Sousa Santos (2007, p. 45) insightfully calls abyssal thinking. That is Modern Western Eurocentric thinking consists of:

> a system of visible and invisible distinctions, the invisible ones being the foundation of the visible ones. The invisible distinctions are established through radical lines that divide social reality into two realms, the realm of "this side of the line" and the realm of "the other side of the line". The

division is such that "the other side of the line" vanishes as reality, becomes nonexistent, and is indeed produced as nonexistent. Nonexistent means not existing in any relevant or comprehensible way of being. Whatever is produced as nonexistent is radically excluded because it lies beyond the realm of what the accepted conception of inclusion considers to be its other. What most fundamentally characterizes abyssal thinking is thus the impossibility of the co-presence of the two sides of the line. To the extent that it prevails, this side of the line only prevails by exhausting the field of relevant reality. Beyond it, there is only nonexistence, invisibility, non-dialectical absence.

(Santos, 2007, p. 45)

By challenging such abyssal logic, *Decolonizing Interpretive Research* indigenously and subalternly confronts the colonizing nature of our field and in so doing confronts the colonized nature of the colonized as well, disassembling a eugenic reason that grants "to modern science the monopoly of the universal distinction between true and false, to the detriment of alternative bodies of knowledge" (Santos, 2007, p. 47). That is, the "exclusionary character of this monopoly is at the core of the modern epistemological disputes between scientific and nonscientific forms of truth established by certain methods" (Santos, 2007, p. 47). That is,

popular, lay, plebeian, peasant, or indigenous knowledges on the other side of the line [vanish] as relevant or commensurable knowledges because they are beyond truth and falsehood. It is unimaginable to apply to them not only the scientific true/false distinction, but also the scientifically unascertainable truths of philosophy and theology that constitute all the acceptable knowledge on this side of the line. On the other side of the line, there is no real knowledge; there are beliefs, opinions, intuitive or subjective understandings, which, at the most, may become objects or raw materials for scientific enquiry. Thus, the visible line that separates science from its modern others is grounded on the abyssal invisible line that separates science, philosophy, and theology, on one side, from, on the other, knowledges rendered incommensurable and incomprehensible for meeting neither the demands of scientific methods of truth nor those of their acknowledged contesters in the realm of philosophy and theology.

(Santos, 2007, p. 47)

Indigenous and subaltern anti-colonial and decolonial interpretive approaches break up with what has been defined as "research"—a segregated Eurocentric concept of geographic time and space barbed-wired by endless prejudices. This argues the need for a de-territorialization, a "Nkrumahanian philosophical consciencism" (Nkrumah, 1964), a collective itinerant commitment that is an organic, fluid, and flexible means of knowing the world, which destabilizes fixed knowledge depictions and absolute beliefs of our time (Paraskeva, 2011, 2016). Darder notes:

decolonizing approaches to research decenter Western-based notions of scientific neutrality, reliability, and validity, by advancing an evolving and itinerant epistemology. This entails a rupturing of Western epistemologies rooted in abstract formulations devoid of both the internal and external negotiations that shape subaltern life, particularly with respect to the most impoverished. This rupturing is an absolute necessary step in that all knowledge is not only not equal, but has had serious consequences for indigenous and subaltern populations.

(pp. 27–28 this volume)

Decolonizing Interpretive Research is a clarion critical anti-colonial call against the positivist scientificity of science (Chapter 1, this volume) that fuels the "coloniality zone." It is a towering itinerant river within the anti-colonial turn. In this sense, it seeks not the post-abyssal, but a non-abyssal, which steams a nonnegotiable *desprendimento* (*total*, one must emphasize). Following Walter Mignolo's (2011) examination of Anibal Quijano's reasoning, *desprendimento* or *desprenderse* (i.e., delinking) implies epistemic de-linking or, in other words, epistemic disobedience.

Epistemic disobedience leads us to decolonial options as a set of projects that have in common the effects *experienced* by all the inhabitants of the globe that were at the receiving end of global designs to colonize the economy (appropriation of land and natural resources), authority (management by the Monarch, the State, or the Church), and police and military enforcement (coloniality of power), to colonize knowledges (languages, categories of thoughts, belief systems, etc.) and beings (subjectivity). "Delinking" is then necessary because there is no way out of the coloniality of power from within Western (Greek and Latin) categories of thought (Mignolo, 2011, p. 45).

Such epistemological disruption is not an overnight plastic metamorphoses fabricated in vacuity and out of the material conditions that petrified the oppressed as a sub-human. In fact, contributors of this volume, through the intellectual leadership and with the solidarity of Darder, dissect and map out graphically the gradual construction of such insubordination and the concomitant awakening of the subaltern voice. That is, decolonizing inter-pretive methodologies, as articulated here by Darder, trigger a tough and painful process of irreversible political clarity, learning to unlearn (Tlostanova & Mignolo, 2012) to deal with the need to open the veins of coloniality, a pro-cess that emerges organically. Hernandez unleashes this pain by writing:

As such, I began to engage more critically with my own experiences in the service learning field; yet, initially, this was difficult to enact as a living praxis. Through a process of reflection and dialogue with others, I became more acutely aware of the oppressive injustices that were at work within the service learning field and even began to articulate them well; but, somehow, I could not actualize this dimension fully in my work. Be it fear, lack of time, or being stuck within the confines of a structure/organization, a part of me was unwilling and tremendously terrified to do the work. I spent about a year in this space, before I came to a place where I was finally willing to let go of the fatalism and fear that was immobilizing me and fueling my inability to embrace change and the unknown.

(p. 40, this volume)

This book is a vivid example not just about the courage and intellectual honesty (as Amilcar Cabral would put it) of a group of indigenous and subaltern scholars—so many times conveniently infantilized and stripped from their own indigeneity and subalternity (Preface, this volume) by reactionary educators both on the right and the left[1]—aggravated with the racialized pastoral "that the only viable research one could engage in were ones that would ultimately require the distanced objectivity of a researcher, a methodology that would facilitate the very disconnection between academics and communities that indigenous and subaltern scholars had worked to resist before entering graduate school" (p. 53, this volume). Needless to mention is how indigenous epistemologies are destroyed. About this Bautista notes here:

the process of epistemicide disqualifies social agents who operate according to indigenous modes of living aligned with indigenous epistemologies. By disqualifying, invisibilizing, and ultimately destroying different ways of knowing, those who commit epistemicide assert the dominance of their own epistemological canon, in order to assert power and privilege.

(p. 56, this volume)

As this book illustrates, indigenous and subaltern individuals and communities refuse to exist out of their own identity, challenging Modern Western Eurocentric dominant and counter-dominant ways to read and justify the real—and dare not to resist but "to re-exist" (Walsh & Mignolo, 2018), a re-existence that can only happen out of the Eurocentric matrix. Such re-existence is, indeed, existence otherwise. We are before a very impressive set of autochthone approaches done by indigenous and subaltern intellectuals that refuse to "dream in the language of the settler, of the oppressor" (Couto, 2008, p. 94) and who seek to embark upon a post-abyssal analectical approach palpable, for instance, of a "clinamen" that exhibits the just epistemological ecology of knowledges (Santos, 2005); not only re-interpreting the world, but fundamentally decolonizing counter-hegemonic interpretations and resistances of the word and the world (Freire, 1985).

Decolonizing Interpretive Research echoes an itinerant educational and curriculum theory and praxis commitment toward "a general epistemology of the impossibility of a general epistemology" (Santos, 2007, p. 67) challenging the "hegemonic entanglements that define, structure and epistemologically inform the European, capitalist, military, Christian, patriarchal, white heterosexist, male globalized politics and praxis of coloniality" (p. 21, this volume). Its itinerant, rhizomic and fluid approach to knowledge production honoring multiple ways of knowing" (p. 99, this volume) is

the prima facie evidence of the indigenous and subaltern intellectual as an epistemological radical, an epistemological pariah, who is challenging and challenged by
a theoretical path that is inexact yet rigorous; s/he "runs away" from any unfor-
tunate "canonology." Such itinerant intellectuality provokes (and exists in a midst
of) a set of crises and produces laudable silences. It provokes an abstinence of theoretical uniformity and stabilization. In this sense, anti-colonial and decolonial
indigenous and subaltern organic intellectuality is a volcanic chain, deeply perpe-
tually a disquiet re-existence (Pessoa, 2014), constantly struggling against the
"vegetal academy of silences" (Pessoa, 2014, p. 270), that forces eugenic "silences
to stop breathing" (Pessoa, 2014, p. 29). By assuming an itinerant flux to decolonize interpretive research, indigenous and subaltern intellectuals show a constant
lack of equilibrium, being always a stranger in his/her own languages. Such itinerant flux is not a sole act, however; it is a populated solitude.

   In echoing this itinerant theoretical posture, Antonia Darder and colleagues
challenge the sociology of absences (Santos, 2014) and how certain non-Western epistemologies have been rendered as non-existent; it challenges any form
of *indigenoustude*; that is, any form of romanticizing of indigenous cultures and
knowledges, without framing this decolonizing discourse in a dichotomy of
West–rest. *Decolonizing Interpretive Research* is not a bastard or misbegotten
approach, nor a dwindling theoretical approach. It is a political commitment
that knows fully well that "the thirst for being complete will push subaltern
reason to a state of useless anguish" (Pessoa, 2014, p. 212). Its deep consciousness of perpetual completeness unveils itinerant beams that "move beyond
the deceptive quantophrenia of positivism—and twisted eurocentric counter
positivist approaches as well—speaking to the understanding and uncritical
tendency not only to embrace quantification of all social phenomena and the
tyrannous discourse of evidence-based" (p. 5, this volume) and above reductive
and unproductive counter-hegemonic ways, challenging positivist dominant
forms of thought.

   That is, decolonizing interpretive research dissected by indigenous and subaltern
scholars should be seen as an itinerant philosophy of praxis, which consciously
assumes that, while Marx was not wrong, the focus should be to transform the
world, "to understand is to destroy oneself" (Pessoa, 2014, p. 63). As an itinerant
process that aims at "not the pleasure, not the glory, not the power, but freedom,
only freedom" (Pessoa, 2014, p. 53), Antonia Darder's *Decolonized Interpretive
Research* challenges both dominant and counter-dominant traditions to respect
three fundamental issues, namely (1) learning that the South exists, (2) learning to
go to the South, and (3) learning from and with the South (Santos, 2014). It is a
commitment to unveil and raise the consciousness built organically to support
transformative social action.

   In this context, decolonized interpretive research also confronts subaltern reason
with dominant and counter-dominant Modern Western Eurocentric epistemologies, a theoretical path of reciprocal and horizontal translation (so crucial within the
processes of coding and decoding) that attempts to prevent the "reconstruction of

emancipatory discourse and practices from falling into the trap of reproducing, in a wider form, Eurocentric concepts and contents" (Santos, 2007, p. xxvi). In so doing, Antonia Darder and colleagues echo Karl Marx (1978), challenging that a real epistemology of liberation and emancipation implies "a ruthless critique of every epistemology that exists"; it is thus a commitment with social, cognitive, intergenerational and spiritual justice done by—as Mia Couto (2008) would put it—indigenous and subaltern *naparamas*, "warriors of justice" (p. 29) and "avengers of the sorrow of the oppressed" (p. 33). In this regard, *Decolonizing Interpretive Research* judiciously assumes an ideological commitment with the production of an epistemology of liberation that requires the liberation of the very own epistemology itself. Its itinerant dynamic pushes the oppressor and the oppressed subject to a pluri(nonnecessary) directional path, thus opening the veins of an oppressive epistemological canon. It is against any canon.

It is, as Darder (2016) argues, "an epistemology of liberation that can persistently challenge structures of authority, hierarchy, and domination in every aspect of life that must be cultivated, nurtured and embodied within the blessed messiness and unwieldy chaos of everyday life within schools and communities" (p. 12). *Decolonizing Interpretive Research*, in the minds of indigenous and subaltern intellectuals, is about reinforcing an anti-colonial river of liberation and emancipation, knowing full well that such struggle is not just "indigenous and subaltern"—it is "the struggle against the mystification and monopoly of Western forms of knowledge cannot fall into the same trap of mysticism" (Paraskeva, 2016).

In unearthing and dissecting the richness of indigenous and subaltern epistemes, Antonia Darder and her colleagues challenge centuries of a eugenic epistemology of blindness, unveiling a "laborious decolonialized methodological process of inquiry" (p. 48, this volume), a destabilizing epistemology that aims to defamiliarize the canonic tradition of monocultures of "scientific" knowledge, towards an epistemology of seeing (Saramago, 2007) that unpacks the cultural politics of coloniality (Chapter 3, this volume), thus challenging the coloniality of power, being, knowledge, and labor (Grosfoguel, 2007; Mignolo, 2000; Quijano, 2000). In doing so, contributors to this volume promote an ideological, itinerant, decolonized, hermeneutical ground, which concomitantly offers a robust theory and praxis in which "to think, is to see" (Pessoa, 2014, p. 72). Such decolonial and anti-colonial hermeneutical itinerant position "does not refuse the past; on the contrary, it assumes and redeems the past by the way it swerves from it. Its potential for post-abyssal thinking lies in its capacity to cross the abyssal lines" (Santos, 2007, pp. xxiii–xxiv), with its foci "not on reason, will, and emotion per se, but within (re)imagination" (Pessoa, 2014, p. 281) of the "conditions for transformative practice and community sovereignty and empowerment" (p. 11, this volume).

As a decolonized and itinerant theoretical position (Chapters 4 and 6, this volume), *Decolonized Interpretive Research* confronts and throws the oppressor and oppressed subjects to a permanent unstable question of "what is there to think?" It pushes one to think in the light of the future as well as to question how "we" can actually claim to really know the things that "we" claim to know, if "we" are not ready specifically to think the unthinkable, to go beyond the unthinkable and master its infinitude. It is to be (or not to be) radically unthinkable to better unlearn one's privilege (Spivak, 1988a). In doing so, one generates new insights, develops a new theory (p. 4, this volume), moves towards "new curriculum, theoretical approaches, knowledge practices or political strategies" (p. 7, this volume) knowing quite well that "the power to create needs a point of support, the crutch of reality" (Pessoa, 2014, p. 216).

Indigenous and subaltern anti-colonial commitment—as this volume demon-strates—is a perpetual duel with the material conditions of a racialized reality that mercilessly oppresses and de-humanizes their agency. Needless to say that deco-lonizing interpretive research implies an itinerant metamorphosis between what is thought and nonthought and unthought, but it is fundamentally about the temerity of the colonization of the non/un/thought within the thought; it attempts to understand how big is infinite, the infinite of thought and action. If one challenges infinity, it is chaos because one is in chaos; that means that the question or questions (whatever they are) are inaccurately de-territorialized and fundamentally sedentary.

Quite sentient of its itinerancy, decolonizing interpretive indigenous and sub-altern scholars promote a new *poesis* that itinerantly throws the subject against the infinite of representation to grasp the omnitude of the real(ity) and the rational (ity), thus mastering the transcendent. It is a *poesis* fleeced not within chaos, but within the healthy cacophonic and reckless rhythm of chaos, since "there is not 'the' chaos, but multiple regimes of chaos" (Gil, 2018, p. 293), regimes that were organically triggered consciously and unconsciously by indigenous and subaltern individuals to face de-humanization propelled by Modern Western Eurocentric epistemologies and its colonialities (Quijano, 2000). Thus, "chaos arises as healthily endemic, and rhythm does not necessarily erupts within the same plane as the rhythm subject; the rhythm of chaos does not transpire a single beat" (Gil, 2018, p. 294) as de-humanization, subalternization, and colonization are not a single beat phenomena. "While the rhythm of chaos reflects a great deal in common with the oppressor, the fact is that it doesn't have a recognized logical cadence, it is also made of silences that participate in the construction of rhythmic regimes of chaos" (Gil, 2018, pp. 294–295).

My argument is that the anti-colonial struggles for a decolonized interpretive research toward a non-abyssal path—as Darder and the contributors of this volume eloquently demonstrate—implies to consciously not alienate such chaos, but to reinforce and re-exist within a rhythm of chaos, since that there is not one single path toward a *poesis* of freedom and emancipation. Chaos, usually eugenically constructed as a synonym and reflection of the underdeveloped condition of indi-genous and subaltern communities, is the supreme condition and basis of struggle against the oppressor. This struggle is characterized by a constant "search for new lines of flight, seeking to construct new realities that, in essence, are artistic and trans-artistic instances" (Gil, 2018, p. 413). This entails a just struggle based on the authority of the oppressed to engage its own oppressed dynamics (Chapter 1, this volume); such struggle for re-existence gushes power dynamics, a massive itinerant *poesis*—thus transformative—through which indigenous and subaltern communities—as artists and goldsmiths of the struggle for freedom and emancipation—"transform into singular signs and images; it is the space-time block where the artist connects his forces with the natural and cosmic forces" (Gil, 2018, p. 413).

Being more *poesis* than just "theory" (and not because it is less theory), the itinerant position of decolonizing interpretive research *epitomizes* a transcendent nomadography (or projection of an alternative line), which is not transcendental. In this sense, it is also "a theory of change" (Spivak, 1988b, p. 3), that goes beyond confrontation as the matrix for change and assumes a commitment to "radical co-presence" (Santos, 2014), or, better said, a subaltern radical co-presence toward a non-abyssal borderless path. It is thus a theory and praxis sentinel, as "the best sentry is to have no borders" (Couto, 2008, p. 17), a praxis that is deeply sentient in a world epistemologically endless and diverse, in which it is impossible to understand reality from one single epistemological position (Santos, 2005). Hence, a successful struggle for social and cognitive, and intergenerational, justice needs to come to grips with the commitment to move way above and beyond both hegemonic and counter-hegemonic Modern Western Eurocentric epistemological terrains (Paraskeva, 2017, 2018).

While "the former openly championed the epistemicide, the latter ended up being incapable of interrupting such epistemicide and, in many ways, ended up helping the scientific and social perpetuation of such anathema. Moreover, in many ways, specific counter dominant traditions were actually crucial enzymes of the epistemicide as well" (Paraskeva, 2018, p. 194). By ignoring for so long the importance of non-Western non-Eurocentric epistemes, most counter-hegemonic Modern Western Eurocentric epistemologies end up being the "epistemicide within the epistemicide" (Paraskeva, 2017, 2018). It is quite incomprehensible how counter-hegemonic movements were/are slow to realize that the solution against epistemicide will never be found in the matrix that produced it, which has made such counter-hegemonic movements not only guilty but also victims. Countless of these victims, such as Karl Marx for example, despite being labeled with certain deficits—"I did not get my post as railway office because of my bad hand-writing"—were not able to think out of a eugenic matrix that annihilated and labeled those outside the classed matrix of privilege as inferior.

The alternatives for the world we wish to see (Amin, 2008) through a social construction of science implies a "decolonizing practice of [science] that genuinely engages the needs of all children in the process of their own education, emancipation, and humanity." However, such political process implies not only to walk away from "traditional reductive methodologies, anchored in Eurocentric values of distanced objectivity and reductive reasoning" (p. 98, this volume), but also, either to walk away or at minimum to monitor non-traditional research approaches sinking irremediably in the bad habits of racialized forms of Eurocentric science.

Decolonizing Interpretive Research challenges epistemic privilege, putting forward a deterritorialized approach, an itinerant theory, and praxis of nonspaces (Auge, 2003), committed to a path beyond fixed theoretical formulations. This is a transgressive posture, which implies that to decolonize interpretive research is "to travel, to go beyond the limits, to move, and stay in a kind of permanent exile" (Said, 2005, p. 41). As theory and praxis of non-places and non-times is, in essence, a theory and praxis of all places and all times. It is a clear call against the precariousness of any fixed theoretical position (Chapters 3, 4, and 6, this volume).

Decolonizing Interpretive Research, employed by indigenous and subaltern organic intellectuals, insightfully recognizes that it is not a laudatory "design of a geography of 'saudade'" (Couto, 2008, p. 76). While "saudade"—epitomized in the words and rhythms of world-renowned Cape Verdean Morna of Cesária Évora—should not be interpreted as an ideological, cultural, or spiritual weapon of the oppressed to contend with centuries of de-humanization. Instead, indigenous and subaltern scholars advocate for the legitimacy of an oppressed reason that challenges the way Eurocentric exoticisms ideologically de-weaponize the cultural and spiritual artillery of the oppressed. "Saudade", indigenously and subalternily, is nurtured as the sentinel of history, given that the oppressed refused to be an object in the "Museum." In doing so, they are quite sentient that the struggle for a just world—although a labor of love, as Jose Marti would put it (1973)—is not an easy one, and history "as long as it is always stolen and narrated by the voice and wrist of the oppressor will always wipe its feet on the back of the oppressed" (Couto, 2008, p. 58). Although aiming toward anti-colonial metamorphoses, indigenous and subaltern scholars who champion a just struggle to decolonize interpretive research know that "one did not yet invent a soft, maneuverable powder, capable of blowing up the human being without killing him … And of the exploded human being [are] born infinite human beings who are inside them" (Couto, 2008, p. 68). While such dynamics of struggle—including class, race, ethnicity, and gender, and categories, such as culture, economy, and politics—are crucial to understand and name the colonial power matrix of Modern Western Eurocentrism, it is undeniable that spirituality cannot be sidelined.

As the promiscuous nexus of concubines, Colonialism and Christianism was a supreme enzyme in the consolidation of instilling heteropatriarchy and racism, rape, colonial educational apparatuses, linguistic genocide, a colonial political economy, a de-humanizing solution that started right at the first encounter between white settlers and indigenous populations (Chapters 3 and 6, this volume). In this sense, *Decolonizing Interpretive Research* is also a commitment to explode the way Eurocentrism reductively frames rationality, being sentient of spirituality—racially ridicularized as voodoo, "feitiçaria," as a structural component within the oppressed saga in the struggle to reason the butchering de-humanization of the oppressor within the physical and metaphysical path. Spirituality is an indigenous and subaltern asset, a root of its revolution, to challenge colonial oppressive religious forms, based on an alarming racist ignorance that indigenous and subaltern communities are destitute of any legitimate forms of physical and metaphysical beliefs, rituals, and utopias. In so doing, indigenous and subaltern are transformative agents, demythologizing hegemonic beliefs—and I would add, counter hegemonic as well—as part of a larger process of empowerment, of a larger imperative for liberation bringing their "own history as colonized subjects to bear upon the manner in which one engages philosophically" and in the process unpack—among other things—how dynamics such as "self-esteem moved from philosophical supposition to a hegemonic construct in mainstream Western culture" (p. 78, this volume).

The struggle against the eugenic commonsensical belief that "beyond the Equator there is no sins" (Santos, 2007) is the sublime example of Eurocentrism as a religious racialized reasoning. It is a struggle against being a "walking contradiction, that is the very faith that one holds dear and to which one has devoted his/her own life, could very well be seen as the same faith used to justify and sustain acts of oppression and injustice toward my ancestors" (p. 106, this volume). In order come to grips with such contradiction and name it (Chapter 1, this volume), indigenous and subaltern scholars need to unpack a fabricated abyssal line between the Scriptures and how "Christianity, has been steeped in dogma, justifying the proliferation of institutionalized racism, classism, sexism, inequality, and many other forms of dehumanization" (p. 106, this volume). Thus, an indigenous and subaltern anti-colonial commitment to decolonize interpretive research is an itinerant claim to un-puzzle the nexus of physical–metaphysical.

In doing so, it brings not just spirituality, but also indigenous and subaltern reason to its just position; one that fuels praxis; one that contends with the oppressor not from an inferior stance. In this sense, it is not a "Westernized paranormal activity", a "xicuembo theory and praxis" (Couto, 2008, p. 45). That is, we are bodies; we are not institutions, although a schizophrenic system institutionalizes us. Thus, such anti-colonial struggle is an ethical take of liberation and emancipation, as Darder rightly argues,

> which encompasses a rethinking of the totality of moral problems from the point of view of the most oppressed. This ethical concern within decolonizing interpretive research mobilized us to (re)define and (re)articulate absences and emergences of knowledge claims from our subalternity, in order set forth decolonizing strategies of engagement for altering current hegemonic discourses and practices in the world, which perpetuate colonizing and economically impoverishing aberrations.
>
> *(p. 30, this volume)*

Organically, indigenous and subaltern scholars reject vehemently the yoke of book worship (Tse Tung, 2007, p. 45) as the sublime source of knowledge construction; on the contrary, they assume a commitment to the multiplicity of forms to read and be in the wor(l)d. It is in this sense, a "praxis of losses, of infinite mourning" (Couto, 2008, p. 105), that goes above and beyond into "la raza cosmica" (Anzaldua, 2007, p. 99), and implies theories of inclusivity, "a new *mestiza* consciousness, *una consciencia de mujer*. It is a consciousness of the borderlands" (Anzaldua, 2007, p. 99). It is a "subaltern social consciousness" (Spivak, 1988b), but not "a dislocated or incoherent social consciousness" (Spivak, 1988a, p. 71). It is a communal process, a collective power of consciousness—or political grace (Darder, 2011). It is people's theory and research praxis, unpacking a *paradigma otro* (a paradigm by the other) that "does not fit into a linear history of paradigms or epistemes [that] runs counter to the greatest modernist narratives [and] reaches towards the possibility of non-European modes of thinking" (Escobar, 2013, p. 34; Mignolo, 2000, 2013).

In this afterword, I have tried to engage more in a "wordwith"—and not a traditional afterword—and to create new streams within our river with the contributors of this volume, a volume that is especially precious under the current viral fascism we are living. In this volume, Antonia Darder, once again, sets an irreversible anti-colonial alternative tone, and shows the field otherwise, by unpacking not the possibility of other knowledges, but dissecting alternative ways of thinking and doing alternatives (Santos, 2005) as real. In keeping with the ethos of this interpretive praxis, Darder rolls up her sleeves and, in *Decolonizing Interpretive Research*, unpacks a decolonial cognitive matrix—pure and raw decoloniality in the making—going above and beyond the liberal commonsense clichés of "hope and possibility," "el camino se faz caminando," that have colonized academia as intellectual folklore.

It is thus, as I have mentioned previously, a sharp act of intellectual honesty of indigenous and subaltern scholars who not only refuse to live on their knees, but have decided to die standing, confronting the oppressor eye-to-eye, and torpedoing its racialized cognitive core. I believe it is time now to make a pause on my "wordwith" my indigenous and subaltern colleagues. Before a noisy silence takes control of such pause, I would like to bring to the village of our ideas, the story of Myrna Mack.

> In the year 2004, for once the government of Guatemala broke with the tradition of impunity and officially acknowledge that Myrna Mack was killed by order of the country's president. Myrna had undertaken forbidden reason. Despite receiving threats, she had gone deep into the jungles and mountains to find exiles wandering in their own country, the indigenous survivors of the military massacres. She collected their voices. In1989, at a conference of socials scientists, an anthropologist from the United States complained about the pressure exert to continually produce: "In my country, if you don't publish you perish". And Myrna replied: "In my country if you publish, you perish". She published. She was stabbed to death.
>
> *(Galeano, 2013, p. 126)*

In an era in which, basically, "if you think you perish," Antonia Darder's long-standing anti-colonial commitment to work communally with indigenous and subaltern students and researchers, assisting them to break up lethargic forms of reified social consciousness, in order to dismantle a classed, racialized, and gendered cognitive empire, must not go unnoticed.

Note

1 We all have been in countless doctoral committees here and abroad and heard from respectful critical scholars harsh criticisms on students, as they have "no authority" to claim their voice without backing up their claims on the research they did. Indigenous and subaltern knowledges and methodologies are not about backing up claims in Modern Western Eurocentric scientific methods and findings. It is actually to challenge the Modern Western epistemological matrix, as well as its findings. To deny this is to perpetuate the epistemicide. Indigenous and subaltern intellectuals committed to the anticolonial struggle to decolonize interpretive research challenge the epistemic violence of Western academic forms (Chapter 1, this volume).

References

Abu-Lughod, J. (1989). *Before European hegemony: The world system A.D. 1250–1350.* New York: Oxford University Press.

Amin, S. (2008). The world we wish to see: Revolutionary objectives in twenty first century. *The Bamako Appeal*, 107–112.

Anzaldua, G. (2007). *Borderlands. La frontera. The new mestiza.* San Francisco: Aunt Lute Books.

Auge, M. (2003 [1994]). *Não-Lugares: introdução a uma antropologia da supermodernidade.* Campinas: Papirus Editora.

Bachelard, G. (2014). *Poetics of space.* New York: Penguin.

Couto, M. (2008). *Terra Sonambula.* Lisbon: LEYA.

Darder, A. (2011). *A dissident voice: Essays on culture, pedagogy, and power.* New York: Peter Lang.

Darder, A. (2016). Ruthlessness and the forging of liberatory epistemologies: An arduous journey. In Joao M. Paraskeva (Ed.), *Curriculum epistemicides.* New York: Routledge, pp. ix–xvi.

Dussel, E. (2013). *Ethics of liberation: In the age of globalization and exclusion.* Durham, NC: Duke University Press.

Eco, U. (2017). *Chronicles of a liquid society.* New York: Harcourt.

Escobar, A. (2013). Words and knowledges otherwise. In W. Mignolo & A. Escobar (Eds.), *Globalization and the decolonial turn.* New York: Routledge, pp. 33–64.

Fanon, F. (1963). *The wretched of the earth.* New York: Grove.

Freire, P. (1985). Reading the word and the world. An Interview with Paulo Freire. *Language Arts* 62(1), 15–21.

Galeano, E. (2013). *Children of the days: A calendar of human history.* New York: Nation Books.

Gil, J. (2018). *Caos e Ritmo.* Lisbon: Relogio D'Agua.

Giroux, H. (2018). *American nightmare: Facing the challenge of fascism.* San Francisco: City Lights.

Grosfoguel, R. (2007). The epistemic decolonial turn: Beyond political economy paradigms. *Cultural Studies* 21(2–3), 211–223.

Harding, Sandra (2008). *Sciences from below: Feminisms, postcolonialities and modernities.* Durham, NC: Duke University Press.

Hedges, C. (2009). *Empire of illusion: The end of literacy and the triumph of spectacle.* New York: Nation Books.

Horkheimer, M., & Adorno, T. W. (2002). *Dialectic of enlightenment.* Stanford: Stanford University Press.

Johnson, C. (2011). *The neoliberal deluge: Hurricane Katrina, late capitalism and the remaking of New Orleans.* Minnesota: University of Minnesota Press.

Judis, J. B. (2016). *The populist explosion: How the great recession transformed American and European politics.* New York: Columbia Global Reports.

Kazin, M. (2017). *The populist persuasion*. Ithaca: Cornell University Press.

Marti, J. (1973). *Nuestra America*. Barcelona: Editorial Ariel.

Marx, K. (1978 [1843]). For a ruthless critique of everything existing. In R. Tucker (Ed.), *The Marx Engels reader*. New York: W. W. Norton, pp. 12–15.

McIntyre, L. (2018). *Post-truth*. Cambridge, MA: MIT Press.

Mignolo, W. (2000). *Local histories/global designs: Essays on the coloniality of power, subaltern knowledges and border thinking*. Princeton: Princeton University Press.

Mignolo, W. (2011). Epistemic disobedience and the decolonial option: A manifesto. *Transmodernity. Journal of Peripheral Cultural Production of the Luso-Hispanic World* 1(2), 44–66.

Mignolo, W. (2013). Introduction: Coloniality of power and decolonial thinking. In W. Mignolo & A. Escobar (Eds.), *Globalization and the decolonial turn*. New York: Routledge pp. 1–21.

Nkrumah, K. (1964). *Consciencism*. New York: Monthly Review Press.

Paraskeva, J. M. (2011). *Cultural studies, power & education*. Lisbon: Pedago.

Paraskeva, J. M. (2016). *Curriculum: Whose internationalization?* New York: Peter Lang.

Paraskeva, J. M. (2017). *Towards a just curriculum theory: The epistemicide*. New York: Routledge.

Paraskeva, J. M. (2018). ¿Qué sucede con la teoría crítica (currículum)? La necesidad de sobrellevar la rabia neoliberal sin evitarla. In Rosa Vasquez Recio (Ed.), *Reconocimiento y Bien Comun en Educacion*. Madrid: Morata, pp. 191–230.

Perelman, M. (2000). *The invention of capitalism: Classical political economy and the secret history of primitive accumulation*. Durham, NC: Duke University Press.

Pessoa, F. (2014). *The book of disquiet*. New York: Penguin Books.

Quantz, R. (2011). *Rituals and students identity in education: Ritual critique for a new pedagogy*. New York: Palgrave.

Quijano, A. (2000). Colonialidad del poder y classificacion Social. *Journal of World Systems Research* 6(2), 342–386.

Said, E. (2005). Reconsiderando a Teoria Itinerante. In M. Sanches (Ed.), *Deslocalizar a Europa. Antroplogia, Arte, Literatura e História na Pós-Colonialidade*. Lisbon: Cotovia, pp. 25–42.

Santos, B. de Sousa (2005). *Democratizing democracy: Beyond the liberal democratic canon*. London: Verso.

Santos, B. de Sousa (2007). *Another knowledge is possible*. London: Verso.

Santos, B. de Sousa (2014). *Epistemologies of the south: Justice against epistemicide*. Boulder: Paradigm.

Saramago, J. (2007) *Seeing*. London: Vintage.

Spivak, G. C. (1988a). Can the subaltern speak? In C. Nelson & L. Grossberg (Eds.), *Marxism and the interpretation of culture*. Chicago: University of Illinois Press, pp. 271–315.

Spivak, G. C. (1988b). Subaltern studies: Deconstructing historiography. In R. Guha & G. Spivak (Eds.), *Selected subaltern studies*. New York: Oxford University Press, pp. 3–32.

Tse Tung, M. (2007). Oppose book worship. In Slavoj Žižek, *Slavoj Žižek presents Mao on practice and contradiction*. London: Verso, pp. 43–51.

Tlostanova, M., & Mignolo, W. (2012). *Learning to unlearn: Decolonial reflections from Euroasia and the Americas*. Ohio: Ohio State University.

Walsh, C., & Mignolo, W. (2018). *On decoloniality*. Durham, NC: Duke University Press.

INDEX

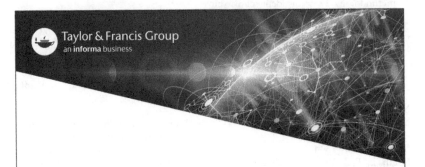